How to Identify
and Care for Houseplants

Houseplants of all kinds grow lushly in the author's garden room. Swedish ivy is at left in a hanging basket; on the shelves there are orchids and bromeliads and on floor level, grape ivy and piggy-back plant. At the right trailing over shelf corner is wandering Jew. (Photo by author)

How to Identify and Care for Houseplants

Jack Kramer

Drawings by Michael Valdez

Doubleday & Company, Inc., Garden City, New York   1975

Library of Congress Cataloging in Publication Data

Kramer, Jack, 1927–
    How to identify and care for houseplants.

    Includes index.
    1. House plants—Identification.   2. House plants.
I. Title.
SB419.K712   635.9′65
ISBN 0-385-02105-4
Library of Congress Catalog Card Number 74–25111

Designed by Mary Frances Nimeck

Contents

Author's Note

Over a period of six years I have grown every plant in this book, and all draw-ings by my patient artist Michael Valdez were done from plants in my garden room or in my home. Photographs can sometimes be deceiving (in glorious color or not), so I chose to use this more simple and sure way to identify houseplants for the indoor gardener.

This room relies on houseplants for its beauty. On shelf at right is kangaroo ivy; under it is bamboo and on the shelf is wandering Jew. The top hanging plant is peperomia and a small-leaved tradescantia below it. (Photo by Clark Photographics)

Introduction: Know What You Grow

In the last five years houseplants have become vitally important in the scheme of daily living. People, young or old, in apartments or houses, are more and more using living plants in their immediate surroundings. Our younger generation may be responsible for this renaissance, or it may be simply a natural return to the soil for all of us. In either case, houseplants are now being grown by more people than at any other time in history. And more people want to know just what they are growing. It is necessary to be familiar with the name of a plant to be able to grow it successfully because, even though there are dozens of houseplant books with good cultural instructions for growing specific plants, without knowing the correct name one is at a loss to find this information.

Also, it is no longer just a question of a philodendron or an ivy; today people want specific plants for specific purposes. This makes good sense be-

A fine specimen of Aglaonema and a very effective pot plant. (Photo by Hort Pix)

Fuchsias bring color into the home and most hybrids are floriferous plants that bloom well in their season. (Photo by author)

Scindapsus aureus is a fine vining plant at home in basket; it can also be grown on a small trellis in a pot. (Photo by author)

cause some plants are ideal for large areas like garden rooms, other plants are fine for windows, and still other plants—miniature types—are best suited for terrariums.

Suppliers have met the demands for houseplants by providing the retail outlet with an assortment of fine new plants as well as improved varieties of old ones. Whether you want a plant as a room accent or to beautify a window, in a terrarium or dish garden, there are innumerable plants for you. And if you are growing plants under lights or need a large plant in a garden room, there are also plants for these purposes; thus, because there are so many plants now (as compared to 1965, when I wrote my first book on houseplants), there needs to be some means for identification, some way to determine the name of the plant so you get the right plant for the right place.

In short, there are three reasons for this new book: You must know the correct name of a plant to (1) grow it properly, (2) to use it in the right place or way, and (3) to get the right plant.

In this book we give you a simple and easy way of identifying specific houseplants by leaf shape, leaf edge, and leaf veining. This is not the technical basis for identifying plants; rather, it is a compilation of my years of experience in how to identify plants by sight (many times from a single leaf). I was unable to include all houseplants, so I selected the most popular plants and those that are easy to grow, including old favorites as well as new ones. (I have not included ferns, palms, or cacti because of space limitations and technicalities within these families. Also, these three plant groups are generally recognizable on sight.)

PART ONE

Plant Selection and Care

Aglaonema has variegated leaves and makes a fine indoor plant. There are many new varieties available. In front are jade trees (Crassula argentea). (*Photo by M. Barr*)

14

1

Where to Find Plants

You may buy plants at a local nursery, a wonderful old-fashioned family operation, a newer patio/garden shop, or, in cities, at a local florist. You may also buy them at one of the department stores or five-and-ten garden centers: Sears, Roebuck and Company, Montgomery Ward, Woolworth's. Or you can find plants at the new shops that specialize in houseplants only. All these plant suppliers operate in different ways (because of necessity). Prices will vary from place to place, so you should do comparative shopping. If you do not find what you want in one place, keep looking; there are many new places for plants these days, as well as mail-order sources.

Nurseries, Patio/Garden Centers, Department Stores

Nurseries specialize in plants of all kinds and offer a very good selection of houseplants at fair prices. Generally, you will find a better assortment here

at holiday times such as Christmas or Mother's Day and so on. Most nurseries will have many of the popular houseplants but not all houseplants, particularly since their primary business is in outdoor plants. However, if you ask for a plant by a specific name (and you can now with this book), I am sure the nursery will try to locate it for you.

In addition, at nurseries, you will find many related items for gardening such as plant foods and insect preventatives as well as containers and sundry items for plants. Soil too is available as are other ingredients for potting plants such as gravel and stones and a host of indoor-gardening needs. Also, at nurseries, help is usually well acquainted with indoor plants (one person generally handles the indoor plants) and can answer questions you may have about specific plants you are growing.

The patio/garden centers may have somewhat higher prices than a large nursery because these are generally large complexes that occupy much land space and thus have high rent. However, stock is usually good here.

The plant departments of such large department stores as Montgomery Ward and Sears, Roebuck and Company offer a large selection of all kinds of plants. They are of good quality, and turnover is fast, so chances of getting a bad plant are small. However, prices may be high except at sale times, which occur several times a year. Watch for such sales in newspapers. Unfortunately, in most of these stores the garden help and advice is anything but good, so you are more or less on your own. In other words, you will have to know something about plants to get the most for your money.

Woolworth's and other five-and-ten stores have house and garden plant sections that have various plants at reasonable prices. These stores are good places for frugal shoppers and, even though plants may not be in tiptop shape, they are still satisfactory. Try to get to the store the day the plant shipment arrives (usually on Thursdays or Fridays, although this varies from city to city) so you can still get plants that are fresh. In such stores it is impossible for employees to water plants carefully or to supply the plants with proper light and in a few days' time good plants may become bad ones. Enough said! Get there early.

Local Florists

Local florist shops are beautiful places, and I admire them. They have lovely flowers and absolutely top plants, but prices are tops too! Buy from

Coleus need plenty of water to grow well and can be grown in baskets for a nice display. (Photo by Joyce R. Wilson)

florists if you like, but remember their stock is limited because of space. However, plants sold are usually of the best quality and if they don't have a specific plant in stock, florist shops will generally be able to order it for you.

Houseplant Stores, Boutiques

In between the fine florist shop and the old-fashioned nursery there is a new category: the houseplant stores and boutiques. The merchandise includes containers, terrariums, and oddments as well as plants. The stores I

have scouted have turned out to be excellent places to buy inexpensive houseplants, and sometimes they stock hard-to-find plants. The owners of these specialty places are generally more interested in plants than the large concern (whose buyer has several departments to care for). As a result, the owner knows his plants by name and knows how to care for them. What is more fortunate is that these growing concerns sell plants at reasonable prices. The markup is rarely over 25 per cent, so you can get a lot for your money. Also, if there is only one plant of a kind, and you express interest in it, do not be surprised if you get a cutting free. (This is not common practice, but it does happen!) Let us hope that these new types of plant stores make the grade because we need the personal touch and the fair exchange.

"Used" Plants

Flea markets are springing up in many areas. These places usually specialize in furniture, but recently I found and bought excellent plants for practically nothing: large cacti for $2.00 and $3.00, philodendrons for $1.00, and a rare contorted ivy species for $2.00, a species that I could never find if I hunted nurseries for years. Do not be finicky about how the plant looks. Even if the mature plant is dead, there will be some offspring—stolons or off-shoots—that can be salvaged, and even if you pay $1.00, you are far ahead of the game.

Garage sales promise to be good hunting grounds for inexpensive plants, but they generally turn out to be less than desirable simply because people are moving, and their plants, like their pets, are valuable and so are the prices. It is better to look elsewhere.

Mail-order Sources

Most mail-order plant suppliers are dependable and want to give you the best so you will order again. These are fine places to buy many kinds of unusual philodendrons or bromeliads; some suppliers have a vast selection. Send for mail-order suppliers' catalogues or listings; you can pick the plant you want, because most catalogues have photographs. Also, prices at mail-order suppliers are less costly than from other sources. This is influenced by

several factors, but the main one is that you get young plants rather than mature ones (from florists, say). And young plants are fine even though you may have to give them more attention at the start than you would a mature plant.

Do not be afraid to have plants sent long distances because, from a reliable dealer, they are well packed and protected and usually arrive in good health. Air freight collect is costly, but plants arrive overnight; check rates with airlines. Parcel post special handling is another way to have plants shipped (moderate in cost), and plants arrive in about five to seven days (depending upon where you live). United Parcel Service is still another way to transport plants; check the yellow pages of the phone book to see if they send to your location.

Other Places for Plants

In addition to the several houseplant sources I have listed, there is still another new group of plant suppliers. These are places similar to the houseplant boutique stores but with a larger selection and a varied inventory of large specimen or decorator plants. These are generally unusual plants with high price tags, but when used as a substitute for furniture to fill a room corner, they are worth the price. These plant companies are presently only in large cities such as Chicago, New York, Los Angeles, St. Louis, and so forth, although I am sure that more of the plant specialty shops will be appearing in other cities too. You will find these companies listed in the yellow pages of your phone book.

How to Tell a Good Plant

Once you know what kind of plant you want and its name, you can shop for plants with an eye for getting your money's worth. And just as there are criteria for buying washing machines and refrigerators, clothing and glassware, there are some general guidelines to lead you to a healthy rather than a sick plant. Look for fresh leaves and perky growth. Observe tips of growing stems to see if the plant is growing; there will be fresh green shoots. Do

A group of Bromeliads: Aechmea, Cryptanthus, Vriesia, and Neoregelia. (Photo by USDA)

This is one of the small Guzmanias showing the flower stalk; leaves are apple green and quite attractive and all in all Guzmanias are easy to care for indoor subjects. (Photo by author)

Maranta is the popular prayer plant and is desirable because of its multicolored foliage. Grows easily in warmth. (Photo courtesy Potted Plant Information Center)

Aechmea fasciata *bears a tufted flower crown that stays colorful for many months. (Photo by author)*

The bromeliad Guzmania zahnii in a driftwood arrangement; the plant is in a pocket of osmunda fiber. (Photo by author)

not buy a plant that has drooping leaves or leaves that are partially yellow or one with limp stems or a wan look.

Also, inspect the soil the plant is in; a caked soil usually means the plant has been around for some time, so it is best to avoid it; any plant that goes without water for a time and has caked soil is bound to have a tougher time adjusting to home conditions than a healthy strong plant. If possible, examine the bottom of the pot to see if roots are coming through the drain hole. If they are, this means that the plant needs repotting and may have been on display a long time; however, it is quite all right to buy the plant if it appears otherwise healthy.

Above all, examine plant foliage to see if there is any evidence of insects. Most of the common ones, such as mealybugs and aphids, are easily recognizable if you look at the leaves carefully and the leaf axils, where insects tend to gather. (See chapter 4 for insect identification and remedies.)

When You Get Plants Home

Do not be too shocked if even the healthiest plant does not fare too well in the first few weeks with you. Grown under ideal conditions, many plants suffer a slight setback when they are shifted into new, sometimes less, optimum conditions. However, in a few weeks most plants regain vigor and start active growth.

When you get your plants home, even if you have examined them closely for insects, it is a good idea to soak the pot to one inch of the rim in a sink of water for about two hours to flush out any hidden insects that may be in the soil. When you see bubbles appearing on the top of the soil, you can remove the plant from the sink.

At first, do not expose the plant to direct sun; gradually move it from a bright place to a brighter place and then finally to a sunny spot. For the first few weeks, observe your plants to see how they are faring. Once the initial adjustment is made, then routine care can be given and less attention is necessary.

2 General Houseplant Care

In essence, growing plants indoors is not terribly difficult if you follow the basic principles of good culture, all of which are discussed fully in the following pages. Occasionally, of course, some plants may not respond but this is more a question of selection than of proper care. Some plants simply never do well indoors no matter how good a gardener you are. Fortunately, the list of these plants is very small and need not worry you.

Temperature and Humidity

Through the years I have found that most (not all) houseplants can be classified into two categories: those that require cool-growing conditions and those that need some warmth to prosper.

Average home temperatures are 64 to 78° F. during the day in winter and 56 to 64° F. at night. In spring and summer, temperatures will be about 10 degrees higher except during dog days, when they may go even higher. Misting and keeping plants cool during hot weather is a must. Ironically, heat will hurt a plant more than coolness. When the temperature reaches 100 in my plant room, the plants suffer, whereas a few cool nights does them little harm. Try to protect most of your plants from intense sun and heat.

Humidity, the amount of moisture in the air, should be at a healthful level for plants and people; a lack of it has been the cause of the demise of many houseplants. An amount of 30 to 40 per cent moisture is fine for most homes and good for most houseplants. If your home does not have a humidifier (usually part of the heating system), you will have to provide additional moisture in the air by setting plants on gravel soaked trays and by misting plants, or by purchasing an inexpensive small humidifier for the room where you keep your plants. Also remember that many plants grown together give off their own humidity.

Plants take up moisture through their roots and release it through their leaves. If the surrounding air is dry, they lose water quicker than they can replace it, and foliage becomes thin and depleted. When summer heat is at its peak, help plants along with a fine-mist spraying. In winter, when artificial heat is high, also provide more moisture in the air.

Ventilation

Most plants like a situation where there is a good circulation of air; they grow better. Do not open windows directly on plants, but be sure some air gets into, and through, the growing area. Always avoid admitting air in cold drafts that blow directly on the plant (or, for that matter, hot air from registers).

If you have air conditioning, you need not worry about plants being too cool as long as the cold drafts are not directed at the plants. A room of, say, 70° F. is fine as long as the night temperature is cooler than the day reading. Plants like and need a temperature difference between day and night. Of course, sometimes this is impossible but generally, through most of the year, temperatures will be less at night than by day.

Soil

A good potting soil is one that is porous and contains all necessary nutrients. Commercially packaged potting soil contains these ingredients but is expensive. A better and less costly soil mixture can be bought by the bushel from greenhouses. In either case, it will be sterilized and contain all necessary nutrients for plant growth.

You can use the soil as it comes from the package or add to it, as the case dictates. For instance, cacti and succulents will need a very porous soil, so add some sand. And any plant will benefit from some leaf mold or humus in the soil. If you want to mix your own soil, use one part soil to one part sand to one part leaf mold. Vermiculite and other "starting mixes" for seeds and cuttings are also at suppliers; so are perlite and gravel.

Nurseries also carry growing mediums that contain no soil; these are generally designated as peatlike mixes. With these mediums, additional feeding is necessary all year, which can be troublesome.

Potting and Repotting

When to shift plants from one pot to another with fresh soil generally puzzles people. But it need not. Repot most medium-sized or smaller plants every year (the nutrients have been used up); larger plants can go two years without new soil. When potting plants, be sure the new container is clean. If it is an old one, scrub it thoroughly with detergent and rinse repeatedly with water. If it is a new one, soak it overnight or the pots will draw undue moisture from the soil of new plantings.

To remove the plant from its old pot, strike the pot edge lightly against a table a few times and then grasp the plant by the collar and jiggle it gently. Tease it from the pot; do not pull it out or you will injure the roots. Crumble away old soil, and trim dead roots (brown ones). The plant is ready for its new container. (If a plant simply will not come out of a pot, it is sometimes better to crack the old pot with a hammer and remove the pieces rather than risk injuring the plant by pulling it harshly.)

To prepare the pot for planting, cover the drain holes (and do use pots with holes) with broken pot pieces (shards). Then spread a layer of porous stone with a few pieces of charcoal to keep soil sweet. Put in a mound of soil, and center the plant; fill in and around the soil. Hold the plant in position with one hand; use the other hand to push the dirt around. Firm the soil around the collar of the plant with your thumbs. Now strike the base of the pot on a table a few times to settle the soil and eliminate air pockets. Leave an inch of space at the top between the pot rim and soil to receive water.

Watering and Feeding

How you water a plant as well as when you water it are both important factors in plants' growth systems. Basically there are two general schedules for watering pot plants. Those in clay pots will need water every third day all year except in winter, when they can be somewhat dry but never cakey. Plants in plastic pots can go longer between waterings because plastic retains moisture longer than clay. If this sounds confusing, just keep soil evenly moist and plants will do fine; soil should never be cakey or soggy.

Learn how to water a plant correctly. This means really watering it so that excess water runs out the drainage holes. Scanty waterings—and many people do this to plants—kill plants over a period of time. Pockets of water develop in the soil while most of the rest of the area is dry. Roots have to reach and crawl for moisture; some do not, and the plants begin to falter.

Use water that is at room temperature. This is not mandatory, but I have found that my plants grow better with tepid rather than icy-cold water which can shock plants. Also, morning watering seems to work better for plants because night watering causes lingering moisture, and coolness at night can result in fungus diseases.

Watering plants is important, but soaking them occasionally to their rims in a sink of water is vital. This dunking leaches out salts that have accumulated in the soil and is an excellent way of making sure all roots get a thorough bath. And because plants breathe through their leaves, wipe foliage with a damp cloth occasionally to keep them clean and to make them look pretty.

More people have questions about giving their plants fertilizers than any other part of plant culture. And consequently feeding plants has become a curse instead of a cure-all. Quite frankly, I feel only very large plants in over ten-inch pots should be fed, and then only with mild solutions through spring and summer and not at all the rest of the year. Plants in pots less than eight inches in diameter should be repotted yearly so they can get fresh nutrients without feeding. If you do feed your plants, use a mild fertilizer, such as 10–10–5, with a light hand.

26

The Growing Cycle

To a great extent, weather is the controlling factor in plant growth even indoors. So as seasons change, so do plant requirements. For example, in spring most plants are starting into growth and need good moisture and growing conditions. Be sure they are getting adequate light and moisture along with regular waterings.

In summer, plants grow rapidly and need plenty of moisture at the roots. Protect them from direct sun, which could be too strong for them. Usually a window screen or a curtain is all that is needed. Mist frequently, keep plants evenly moist, and feed now if you want to.

In fall, with changing weather—some hot days and some cool ones— watering must be done with more care. Watch the weather. If it is cool and gray, forget watering. If it is mild and bright, continue as you would water in summer. Use your common sense to help your plants, and you will be surprised at how they will grow.

In summer, if it is possible, many houseplants benefit from an outdoor session. With natural light and rain water they will prosper. Move them out to a patio or porch when the weather is warm and settled, and bring them indoors soon after Labor Day, before it gets too cool.

You will find that many plants rest in winter. This is natural. There is little growth or flowering. Gradually reduce watering and just keep soil barely moist through the dreary days.

Words to the Wise

People talk to their children to make them behave, to their pets to make them listen, and to their plants to make them grow. I suppose the idea is psychologically good, but between you and me, a plant will grow whether you talk to it or not, so let your conscience be your guide. Perhaps Mother Nature talks to her plants in one way or another, but I doubt if we humble humans should assume such a grandiose role. I have grown over a thousand plants through the years and never talked to any of them, and, as a matter of fact, none ever talked to me!

This handsome leaded-glass terrarium is home for ivy and peperomia. In right corner is a jewel orchid. (Photo by M. Barr)

3

Plants at Home

Terrarium Plants

Terrariums are tremendously popular for growing small plants. In closed, or partially closed, containers—glass or plastic—plants are in a protected environment and usually do not need water for many months—a convenience for most busy indoor gardeners. Also, a terrarium garden is a little world on its own where many plants together create a lovely indoor scene for table or window, or almost any place in the home.

Small plants are the key to success in growing lovely little greeneries. For the most part use miniatures. Prepare the soil base as follows: a layer of pebbles to absorb excessive moisture, some charcoal chips to keep the soil sweet, and at least three or four inches of good rich soil. Place large plants in the rear of the terrarium, medium ones in the middle, and smaller ones in the front. Clothe the rest of the soil with ground-cover-type plants: very tiny-leaved ones. Try to plant in an arc arrangement, with center section open for viewing.

If you are growing plants in a closed case, you will rarely have to give water to plants because the principle of terrariums is that they supply their own moisture. Leaves give off moisture that forms as condensation on the glass and rolls down into the soil. This process repeats itself daily. If the inside of the glass becomes too condensed (you cannot see the plants), remove the lid, cover, or stopper a few hours a day. The trick with closed cases is to be "cruel": Never apply water. If you do, the plants will quickly rot.

Keep closed terrariums out of direct sun but in bright light. In direct sun the inside of the terrarium will become like an oven and the plants will bake. Keep the garden cool and bright. If you are growing a woodland scene, shade and coolness is the rule.

Do not feed plants in terrariums; you want them to stay small, so feeding is not necessary.

If you are growing plants in a partially open container, such as a bubble bowl, goldfish bowl, or openmouthed bottle, you will have to water the soil about once a week or once every second week. However, apply just a *little*

Begonias enjoy the humidity of a closed bubble terrarium and grow rapidly in this situation. The terrarium makes a splendid indoor accent for table or desk. (Photo by M. Barr)

30

A kitchen windowsill with an assortment of small houseplants: Swedish ivy, Chlorophytum, Philodendron, and others. (*Photo by Clark Photographics*)

moisture because most terrariums do not have drainage facilities. Excess water will accumulate at the bottom of the soil and turn it sour, and then plants will eventually rot.

Rarely are plants in terrariums attacked by insects, but if they are, use old-fashioned remedies as described in chapter 4.

Window Plants

Plants at windows may be dieffenbachias or philodendrons, pileas, peperomias or many more. In any case, general care involves, as explained in chapter 2, a good potting soil that is evenly moist and, in some cases, a means of providing humidity for the plants. Pebble trays and misting will help to some degree. Window plants should be chosen with an eye on symmetry; many plants are ungainly and straggly, so select well-rounded, bushy types. Never be afraid to trim and prune plants as necessary to keep them attractively shaped and groomed.

31

The plant stand in the corner is an effective way of accommodating many plants in a small space. Orchids are on the shelves with Aeschynanthus (the lipstick vine). On floor at left is a red coleus. (Photo by author)

In spring, fall, and winter, plants can take full light at windows, but in summer provide them with some protection from hot sun. A screen or a thin curtain is all that is necessary. In very cold winter areas, protect plants by putting some newspapers between the panes and the plants, or move the plants farther back from the window.

A completed dish garden with ivy and peperomias; houseplants come to life in tiny nature scenes like this. (Photo by M. Barr)

Dish gardens are another way to use small houseplants to advantage. Orchids are the predominate plants here. (Photo by author)

Dish Gardens

Dish gardens are those wonderful diminutive replicas of nature you see in trays or dishes, or, for that matter, any container. Similar to terrariums, dish gardens depend upon landscape arrangements to really make them beautiful. All sorts of scenes from nature can be duplicated with a dish garden, and there are hundreds of plants to use. For planting, follow the guidelines outlined in the terrarium section, but remember that although terrariums can supply their own moisture, dish gardens need more attention.

Water plants at least twice a week, and always be sure soil is moist to the touch but never soggy and, of course, never bone dry. Average home temperatures will suit most plants, and a bright location is fine for dish gardens, although in winter some sun is beneficial for plants.

The beauty of dish gardens is that, like terrariums, they are portable and can be used any place in the home as a decorative accent. And the arrangement of many plants together always looks better than a solitary plant at a window.

Specimen Plants

These are the large expensive plants—*Ficus benjamina,* dieffenbachias, dracaenas—that you see in room interiors in lovely magazine ads. (A well-chosen floor plant can do wonders for your rooms too.) These plants, like window plants, need somewhat more care than plants in terrariums.

Generally, specimen plants will need a good amount of water at all times except in winter, when watering can be decreased to about once every ten days. When you water these plants (about once a week), *really* water them. They require a thorough soaking, not just a scanty watering that will form pockets in the soil. Excess water should drain out of the drain holes into the saucers.

Most of the year, except in winter, specimen plants need all the light you can give them. If they are away from windows, be sure they have some artificial light (incandescent or fluorescent) for at least twelve hours a day. Even the best houseplants will not survive without some light, so do be sure to remember that some type of light is absolutely necessary. Because these plants cost as much as a piece of furniture, it pays to give them good care.

Specimen plants are in large pots and difficult to repot, so feed plants every other week with a weak solution of 10–10–5 fertilizer. Repot every second year; this may involve breaking the existing pot so the plant roots are not injured. It takes two people to repot a seven-foot living-room plant, so be prepared and do it right and with great care. Every other month, or at least every six months, try to move the big plant outdoors where you can leach out from the soil the excess salts that sometimes accumulate from feeding. Let the hose run into the soil for at least thirty minutes. This is absolutely necessary to keep room plants in good health.

Most window plants will tolerate some drafts, but the floor plant seems more susceptible to drafts from hot-air registers and air conditioners. Keep large plants out of drafts but in areas of good air circulation. Few plants will grow in a stagnant atmosphere.

Combat insects if they attack plants as described in chapter 4.

Hanging Plants

This type of gardening has become very popular and with good reason. Plants at eye level are easy to see and are in a good position to enjoy good air circulation and good light. Indeed, a well-grown hanging plant is really a beautiful display. But all things of beauty do not come easily, and hanging plants are no exception. They involve a good deal of care, but every effort is worth it for the results: They can make a room sing with color. Cascading plants flow over pot rims and make a veritable fountain of greenery, so try to use them rather than upright growers.

Containers for hanging plants are as yet not as sophisticated as other garden devices (for example, seed tapes and self-watering pots). The terra-cotta pot with attached saucer works well, but so far this is the only container that has an attached drip saucer. For ornamental containers (glazed or pottery), you will have to devise some sort of tray to catch excess water. Be aware, and shop wisely when selecting pots for hanging plants.

Because they are exposed to good air circulation, hanging plants will need more water than most indoor plants. In summer they may require water as often as three times a week. Also give hanging plants good light and some sun (at least two hours a day) to really make them look handsome.

Feed plants as suggested for window plants, and above and beyond all be

Grape ivy are excellent trailing plants and grow easily even with north light. These plants are only nine months old. (Photo by Joyce R. Wilson)

Begonia foliosa *makes a fine hanging plant, and mature specimens like this are stunning. This plant is over two years old. (Photo by Roche)*

Leaves that have a metallic sheen make Episcias desirable, colorful plants. There are many varieties. (Photo by author)

sure that you have suitable strong chain and eye hooks in ceiling for hanging plants. A ten-inch pot filled with soil weighs a considerable amount, and I am always nervous when I sit in restaurants with hanging plants above my head that are supported by flimsy hardware. Be sure your supports and hardware for hanging plants are first-rate.

Since hanging plants grow rapidly and are lavish, they make an ideal dinner for insects of all sorts. Be ever on the alert and use the necessary precautions (chapter 4).

Artificial light will bring African violets to perfection; this is a two-lamp 40-watt setup with reflectors. (Photo by M. Barr)

Artificial Light for Plants

Growing plants under artificial light has gained legions of followers in the last five years. And this is indeed an excellent way to have plants in homes or apartments where natural light is at a minimum. Almost any kind of plant can be grown with artificial light and today there are several different sources of light: fluorescent, incandescent, mercury vapor, quartz. Generally, most people use fluorescent tubes; some of these are specifically designed for plant growth. Incandescent lighting of plants is gaining popularity too and these are also made especially for plant growing. Even a single incandescent lamp (the kind you read by) can help keep plants growing.

Begonias of all kinds make excellent houseplants; an angel-wing is at left and a rhizomatous type at right. Incandescent light helps to keep them growing. (Photo by Guy Burgess)

Fluorescent light has essential blue rays that make foliage grow well and incandescent light is rich in red and far-red rays, also essential to plant growth. Many people use a combination of these sources of artificial light for their plants. Factors such as light intensity, duration, temperature, humidity, and ventilation must all be considered too.

Fluorescent lamps include those made especially for growing plants such as Plant Gro and Gro-Lux. Other fluorescent lamps—the standard types—can also be used and come in a variety of lengths and intensities and qualities of light and are designated cool white, daylight, and so forth. I have found cool white to be quite satisfactory for most plants. Foliage plants require about 15 watts per square foot while flowering plants may need as much as 30 to 35 watts per square foot of space. A good indicator of whether a plant is getting enough light is the plant itself. If it is growing leggy it needs more light; if leaves are faded it is getting too much light. Use artificial light ten to thirteen hours daily.

As mentioned you can use a standard incandescent lamp to help plants or you might want to invest in the new incandescent lamps made especially for plants. This is a bulb that fits into any porcelain socket-type fixture, or special fixtures are available too. Floodlamps for lighting plants are also available. With incandescent lamps keep plants about thirty-six inches from the source of light to eliminate leaf burn. Fluorescent lamps are generally placed four to eight inches from tops of plants.

More sophisticated lighting for plants is also available at suppliers. A lamp with both fluorescent and incandescent elements in the same housing is manufactured by the Duro-Test Corporation and is called Fluomeric and is termed a mercury vapor lamp.

4

Houseplant Problems

Here is a section I hope you do not have to refer to often, but if you follow the few rules outlined earlier, I doubt if you will have to. If you take care of your plants regularly, as you would furniture, appliances, rugs, or carpets, you should have few troubles. But since no one is perfect, this section is included.

Keeping Plants Healthy

To avoid problems, there are a few good rules to follow:
1. Observe plants frequently to determine if trouble is at hand in form of insects, dead leaves, and so on.
2. Keep plants well groomed: Pick off dead leaves and faded flowers before fungus infections can start.

3. Wipe or mist foliage once a week; this cleansing eliminates insect eggs and discourages pests.
4. Dunk plants to pot rims in a sink of water at least once a month.
5. Keep plants out of direct drafts and away from heat and air-conditioner outlets.
6. Repot plants yearly with fresh soil.

Is It You or the Plant?

Many times a plant declines because of poor culture rather than insects or disease. First look to yourself as the culprit before you run out for sprays and remedies. Have you maintained good humidity for plants, watered regularly, and so forth as we have discussed? If plants do not get proper care, there are symptoms:

SYMPTOMS	POSSIBLE CAUSES
Brown or yellow leaves	Too high heat; soil too wet or dry
Yellow or white rings on leaves	Cold water
Leaf drop	Temperature extremes
Pale leaves, weak growth	Too little light
Slow growth	Poorly drained soil
Bud drop	Grown too hot or cold
Collapse of plant	Extreme heat or cold
Crumbly leaves, brown at edges	Too high heat; not enough humidity

Once you have eliminated poor culture, and plants still decline, start looking for insects. The problem is that some of them are minute and you will not see them, but once again there are clues:

CONDITION	POSSIBLE CAUSE
Leaves deformed	Thrips
Plants stunted	Aphids
Leaves gray or brown or crumbly	Red spider
Undersize foliage, spindly growth	Mealybugs

42

Plants lose vigor	Scale
Holes in leaves	Slugs/snails
Leaves gray or yellow	Bacterial blight
Leaves coated white	Botrytis blight

Remedies

If plants do have insects, and you can see most (except red spider), do not run out for chemical poisons. There is no need to use them in the home because there are other and better remedies to eliminate pests. One of the easiest ways to avoid poisons at home is to use a solution of laundry soap and water to spray or douse plants. Mix a one-pound bar in some boiling water and let it dissolve; then add five gallons of water, and you have a solution that will eradicate many houseplant pests. Use the spray once or twice a week until insects are gone.

Plain rubbing alcohol will deter some pests too, notably aphids. Simply use a Q-tip dipped in alcohol and paint insects. They will quickly die. Scale too will be eradicated with this method. Beer placed in bottle caps will get rid of snails, and hot water (90° F.) poured over soil will chase away spring-tails from plants.

Red spiders are persistent devils, and for these you will have to wash plants repeatedly in a soap-and-water solution or else resort to a miticide such as Dimite (if necessary). Use Dimite with caution in the home.

Nicotine sulfate, not classed as an accumulative poison but still potent, eliminates a number of plant insects, but a solution of old tobacco (from cigars or cigarettes) steeped in water a few days and then swabbed on plants will do the same thing.

For mildew outbreaks, use powdered charcoal; for fungus disease, I am afraid you will have to discard plants or else use a poison such as Zineb or Karathane.

PART TWO

More Than 200 Plants to Know

How to Use the Identification Drawings

To identify a plant, first refer to the master key drawings found on the following three pages. For example, look at the shape of the leaf on your plant. Is it oval, heart-shaped, spear-shaped, or so on? Refer to Master Key No. 1 (leaf shapes). Now note the leaf edge—whether it is serrated, plain, or what. Master Key No. 2 helps you identify the leaf edge. Finally, note the leaf veining, and then compare it with Master Key No. 3 (leaf veining). In other words, you are matching numbers: heart shape is No. 1 in Master Key I, smooth leaf edge is No. 1 in Master Key II, and palmate leaf veining is No. 2 in Master Key III. Thus, the code is 1-1-2. Refer to the drawing that has this code in the center of the top of the page. This page will give you the botanical name of the plant you are seeking or trying to properly grow. (There is also a cross-reference, common-botanical-name index chart in the appendix of this book).

I have also included flowers in the drawings to help you further identify the plants and, because some plants are very similiar in leaf or flower characteristics, I have also included silhouettes of a plant's growth habit. Opposite the drawing is specific information on caring for the plant and advice on how it might best be used in the home.

A Word about Plant Names

Plant names may be confusing or simple, depending on how you approach it. Each plant family is divided into one or more families called genera (singular, genus) and in each genus there are generally several species. For example, Philodendron is the genus. In this genus there are many philodendrons, so the species name *cordatum* makes it specific: i.e., *Philodendron cordatum*. An easy analogy is to take your name. Your last name corresponds to the genus name, your first name to the species name. Say, you are Roger Smith. Smith is the genus (family) name, and Roger is the specific or species name.

So far plant names seem fairly easy, but more is involved. Many nurseries specialize in plant breeding, that is mating the best with the best to produce a superior plant. These plants have special names following the species name which simply means they are improved hybrids. For example,

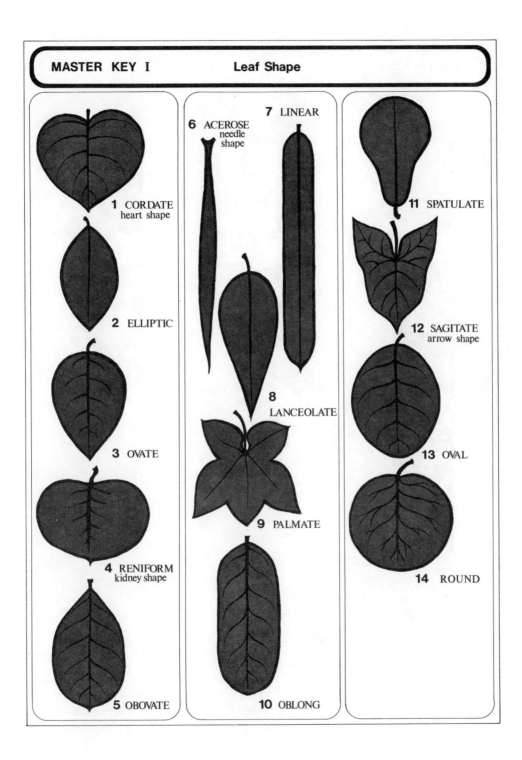

MASTER KEY I   Leaf Shape

1 CORDATE heart shape

2 ELLIPTIC

3 OVATE

4 RENIFORM kidney shape

5 OBOVATE

6 ACEROSE needle shape

7 LINEAR

8 LANCEOLATE

9 PALMATE

10 OBLONG

11 SPATULATE

12 SAGITATE arrow shape

13 OVAL

14 ROUND

1 ENTIRE
smooth edge

2 REPAND

3 SINNATE

4 SERRATE

5 DENTATE

6 CRENATE

7 DEEPLY
LOBED

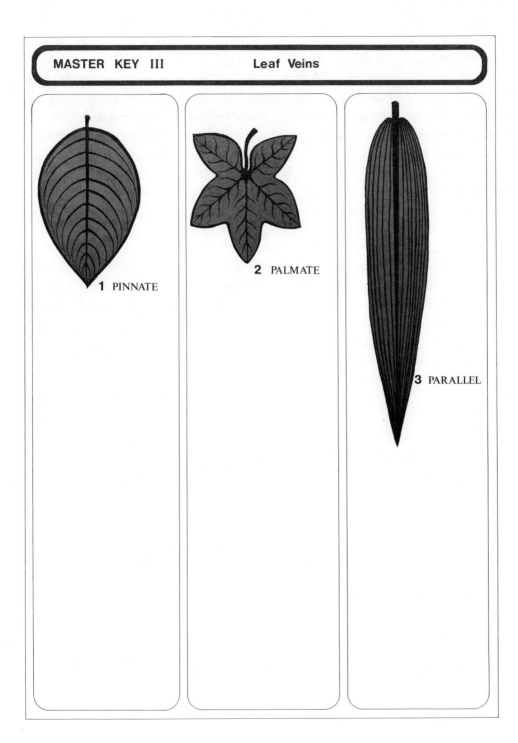

MASTER KEY III   Leaf Veins

1 PINNATE

2 PALMATE

3 PARALLEL

Peperomia caperata 'Golden Ripples.' You can identify these plants because the hybrid name is in single quotation marks.

Most indoor gardeners identify plants by common name rather than by botanical name. For a start, this is fine but it does offer room for error because common names may differ from one region to another. In some areas, *Chlorophytum elatum* is the spider plant, in other locales the friendship plant, and it may also be called airplane plant by many people. So if you are buying or ordering plants by mail for example, common names are no guarantee you will get the plant you want. Botanical names (those tongue-twisters you want to avoid) are the same worldwide so you can order from any catalogue or purchase plants by name from any knowledgeable source and get exactly what you want.

Many times, common names refer to all plants in one plant group (genus). Sansevieria, no matter what its species name, is generally referred to as mother-in-law tongues, or snake plants although there are many species in the group. In this book we have used botanical names (you must start somewhere), but I have included cross-reference listings in the appendix, so you can find the plant by the common name too.

As mentioned, plant breeders hybridize plants and new ones appear frequently. Since plants have been crossbred so many times, leaf shape and edges may vary somewhat in some plant groups. So will leaf size and color. Usually, the dominant leaf shape—oval, heart-shaped, and so forth—remains the same but some variation in edges or size may occur.

Plant Care

In the following plant-care listings, I have tried to keep terms such as the kind of light for a plant and how much water as simple as possible. To further help, the terms are defined below:

Sun: At least three to five hours of sun daily.

Bright: Natural light (near a window) but not sun, although a few hours of sun would be satisfactory.

Shade: Shaded light or light at a north exposure or in an interior place such as a plant on a table or desk.

For watering terms, the following applies:

Keep soil evenly moist: A soil moist to the touch at all times.
Water thoroughly: allow to dry out before watering again:
> Soak soil thoroughly and then wait until it is damp to the touch before watering again.

Plenty of water: Keep soil almost wet at all times.
Keep plants somewhat dry: Soil should be barely moist to the touch.

Where there are exceptions to the above watering methods, notes are made for specific plants.

Size of plants can be confusing to the average indoor gardener and sizes given here refer either to vertical growth or to diameter. Further distinctions are made for trailing plants and vining ones, and true vines are marked accordingly.

There are also propagating notes included for some plants listed under "Remarks." The methods of reproduction include: tip cuttings, slips, crown division, growing new plants from offshoots, or offsets, and from runners. With slip or tip cuttings, place the cutting in a glass of water in a shady place. Crown division is done by separating a large plant. Offsets or offshoots (words used interchangeably) appear at the base of mature plants and when they are 3 to 4 inches tall they can be cut (with a sterile knife) from the parent plant and potted separately in vermiculite or sand-and-soil mix. "Runners," like cuttings, can be rooted in clear water.

Finally, humidity and temperature ranges for plants are cited and are self-explanatory.

PHILODENDRON SCANDENS
1-1-1

Description: Thin, glossy green,
heart-shaped leaves.
Size: To 36 inches.
(Vining.)
Temperature: 55–75° F.
Humidity: 20–30 per cent.
Watering: Keep soil evenly moist.
Light: Bright.
Remarks: Fair trailers; similar to
P. oxycardium.

ANTHURIUM ANDRAEANUM
(flamingo flower)   1-1-1

Description: Green foliage; red,
white, coral, or pink
flowers.
Size: To 16 inches.
Temperature: 65–80° F.
Humidity: 80 per cent.
Watering: Keep soil evenly moist.
Light: Shade.
Remarks: From Central and
South American
jungles. Striking
foliage and winter and
spring "lacquered"
flowers make superb
indoor decoration.

SCINDAPSUS PICTUS
ARGYRAEUS
(ivy arum)   1-1-1

Description: 6-inch satiny green
leaves edged with
silver.
Size: To 36 inches.
(Vining.)
Temperature: 55–75° F.
Humidity: 20–30 per cent.
Watering: Keep soil evenly moist.
Light: Bright.
Remarks: Good vine for
apartment windows;
can take abuse.

52

Anthurium andraeanum

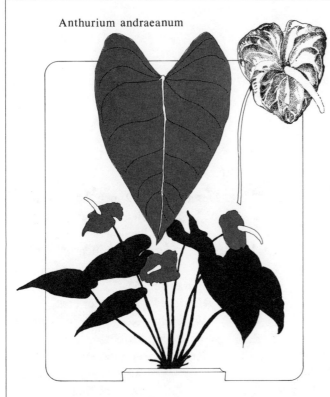

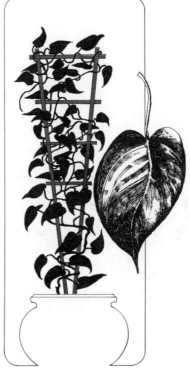

Philodendron scandens

Scindapsus pictus argyraeus

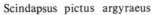

CEROPEGIA WOODII
(rosary vine)   1-1-1

Description: Heart-shaped leaves on trailing threadlike stems; pink or purple blooms with small tubers at the ends of the stems.
Size: To 20 inches. (Trailing.)
Temperature: 55–60° F.
Humidity: 30–40 per cent.
Watering: Let soil dry out between waterings.
Light: Sun.
Remarks: Grows best in airy place. More bizarre than beautiful, this is a novelty.

SCINDAPSUS AUREUS
(ivy arum)   1-1-1

Description: 12-inch dark green leaves laced with yellow.
Size: To 36 inches. (Vining.)
Temperature: 55–75° F.
Humidity: 20–30 per cent.
Watering: Keep soil evenly moist.
Light: Bright.
Remarks: A good vine for an apartment. New plants from cuttings.

PHILODENDRON ASPERATUM
1-1-1

Description: Large heart-shaped corrugated leaves.
Size: To 5 feet. (Vining.)
Temperature: 55–75° F.
Humidity: 20–30 per cent.
Watering: Keep soil evenly moist.
Light: Shade.
Remarks: Splendid decorator plant for room corners.

Ceropegia woodii

Scindapsus aureus

Philodendron asperatum

PHILODENDRON SODIROI
1-1-1

Description: Dark green, heart-
shaped leaves;
semivining.
Size: To 60 inches.
(Branching.)
Temperature: 60–75° F.
Humidity: 20–30 per cent.
Watering: Keep evenly moist.
Light: Shade.
Remarks: An excellent
overlooked
philodendron; stellar
accent plant.

PHILODENDRON OXYCARDIUM
1-1-1

Description: 10-inch leaves.
Size: To 36 inches.
(Vining.)
Temperature: 55–75° F.
Humidity: 20–30 per cent.
Watering: Keep soil evenly moist.
Light: Shade.
Remarks: The most popular
philodendron; a
clambering-vine type.

FICUS PUMILA
(creeping fig)   1-1-1

Description: 1-inch leaves. Often
used as a soil cover for
big pot plants.
Size: To 10 inches.
(Vining.)
Temperature: 60–75° F.
Humidity: 20–30 per cent.
Watering: Keep soil evenly moist;
dry out somewhat in
winter.
Light: Bright.
Remarks: Good creeper;
charming window
plant.

HOMALOMENA RUBESCENS
1-1-1

Description: Reddish-green heart-
shaped leaves with
red-brown edges.
Size: To 48 inches.
Temperature: 65–75° F.
Humidity: 30–40 per cent.
Watering: Keep soil evenly moist.
Light: Shade.
Remarks: Good indoor plant for
very shaded areas such
as a north window.

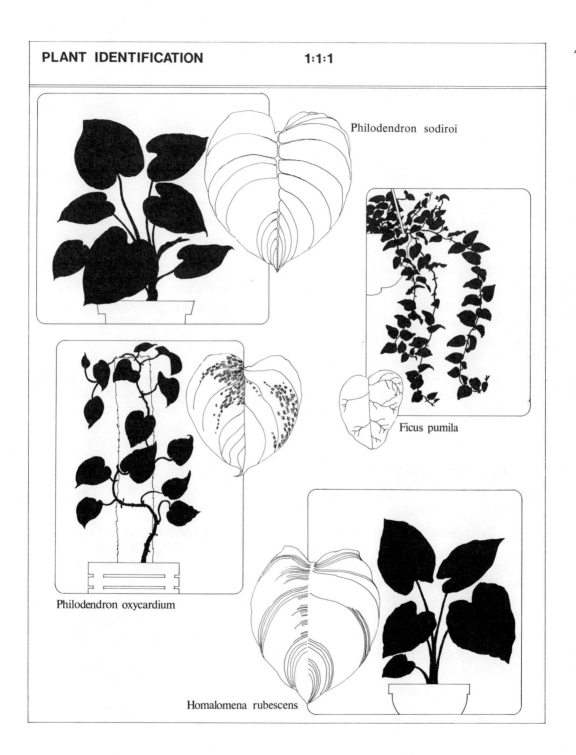

Philodendron sodiroi

Ficus pumila

Philodendron oxycardium

Homalomena rubescens

PEPEROMIA MARMORATA
'SILVER HEART'
1-1-2

Description: Heart-shaped rich
green leaves.
Size: To 18 inches.
Temperature: 55–75° F.
Humidity: 20–30 per cent.
Watering: Keep soil evenly moist.
Light: Bright.
Remarks: A very colorful and
robust small plant.

PEPEROMIA VERSCHAFFELTI
1-1-2

Description: Heart-shaped bluish-
green leaves with
silver bands.
Size: To 18 inches.
Temperature: 55–75° F.
Humidity: 20–30 per cent.
Watering: Keep soil evenly moist.
Light: Bright.
Remarks: One of the best; a
symphony of color and
almost impossible to
kill.

PEPEROMIA CAPERATA
'EMERALD RIPPLE'
1-1-2

Description: Heart-shaped,
corrugated deep green
leaves.
Size: To 14 inches.
Temperature: 55–75° F.
Humidity: 20–30 per cent.
Watering: Keep soil evenly moist.
Light: Bright.
Remarks: One of the best and
most colorful
peperomias for
terrariums or windows.

PEPEROMIA CAPERATA
'TRICOLOR'
1-1-2

Description: Corrugated milky-
green leaves with
white markings.
Size: To 18 inches.
Temperature: 55–75° F.
Humidity: 20–30 per cent.
Watering: Keep soil evenly moist.
Light: Bright.
Remarks: Another excellent
small houseplant. New
plants from stem
cuttings.

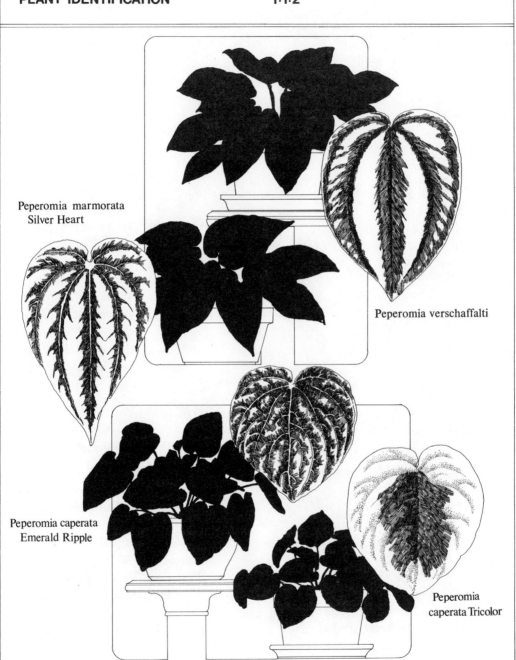

Peperomia marmorata
Silver Heart

Peperomia verschaffalti

Peperomia caperata
Emerald Ripple

Peperomia
caperata Tricolor

ALOCASIA SEDENI
1-2-1

Description: Leaves purple beneath
and veined white
above.
Size: To 36 inches.
Temperature: 60–75° F.
Humidity: 70–80 per cent.
Watering: Plenty of water.
Light: Shade.
Remarks: Ornamental and
variegated foliage.
Use crown division
with plants to get new
ones.

ALOCASIA LOWII GRANDIS
1-2-1

Description: Metallic brown-green
foliage.
Size: To 24 inches.
Temperature: 65–75° F.
Humidity: High humidity, to 80
per cent.
Watering: Keep soil evenly moist.
Light: Shade.
Remarks: Dramatic exotic, with
heart-shaped leaves
high on thin stems.
Needs good drainage.

CALADIUM 'ANN GREER'
1-2-1

Description: Big red-bronze leaves
with emerald tracings.
Size: 20–30 inches.
Temperature: 60–70° F.
Humidity: 60–70 per cent.
Watering: Plenty of water.
Light: Shade.
Remarks: Keep out of sun. Rest
every three months
with very little water,
then start in fresh soil.

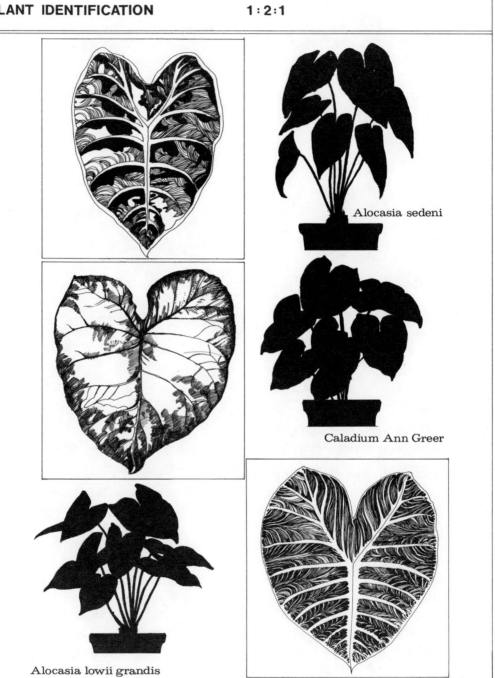

Alocasia sedeni

Caladium Ann Greer

Alocasia lowii grandis

PHILODENDRON PERTUSUM
(Swiss-cheese plant)   1-7-1

Description:	Juvenile form of *Monstera delicosa;* bright green, roundish leaves.
Size:	To 30 inches. (Branching.)
Temperature:	55–75° F.
Humidity:	20–30 per cent.
Watering:	Keep soil evenly moist.
Light:	Bright.
Remarks:	Tends to be straggly, but very easy to grow.

PHILODENDRON SELLOUM
1-7-1

Description:	Dark green, 24-inch, pendent leaves.
Size:	To 60 inches. (Vining.)
Temperature:	55–75° F.
Humidity:	20–30 per cent.
Watering:	Keep soil evenly moist.
Light:	Bright.
Remarks:	One of the self-heading philodendrons; a fine room plant.

Philodendron pertusum

Philodendron selloum

FICUS BENJAMINA
(weeping fig)   2-1-1

Description: A dense head of gracefully pendent drooping branches.
Size: To 5 feet.
Temperature: 60–75° F.
Humidity: 20–30 per cent.
Watering: Keep soil evenly moist; dry out somewhat in winter.
Light: Bright.
Remarks: A small tree, with 2-inch oval leaves. An almost perfect house-plant.

STEPHANOTIS FLORIBUNDA
(Madagascar jasmine)   2-1-1

Description: Scented waxy-white flowers in June, July, and August, with dark green leathery leaves.
Size: To 15 feet, but can be kept small. (Vine.)
Temperature: 50–75° F.
Humidity: 30–50 per cent.
Watering: Water about three times a week except in winter, when once a week is enough.
Light: Bright.
Remarks: A handsome vine. Root cuttings in spring for new plants.

RUELLIA MAKOYANA
2-1-1

Description: Silver-veined leaves; carmine flowers.
Size: To 18 inches.
Temperature: 60–75° F.
Humidity: 30–40 per cent.
Watering: Keep soil barely moist.
Light: Sun.
Remarks: Colorful and dependable for winter bloom.

RUELLIA MACRANTHA
2-1-1

Description: Dark green leaves; rose-colored blooms.
Size: To 40 inches.
Temperature: 60–75° F.
Humidity: 30–40 per cent.
Watering: Keep soil barely moist.
Light: Sun.
Remarks: Dependable and colorful plant for winter bloom.

Ficus benjamina

Stephanotis floribunda

Ruellia makoyana

Ruellia macrantha

CODIAEUM GLORIOSUM
(croton)   2-1-1

Description: Striking multicolored foliage of large, broad, red-purple-maroon leaves.
Size: To 3 feet.
Temperature: 60–80° F.
Humidity: To 70 per cent.
Watering: Keep soil evenly moist except in December and January.
Light: Sun.
Remarks: Splendid accent plant. Needs good air circulation.

CITRUS TAITENSIS
(dwarf orange tree)   2-1-1

Description: Dark green and shiny foliage; attractive branching habit.
Size: To 6 feet.
Temperature: 55–60° F.
Humidity: 20–30 per cent.
Watering: Water heavily when plant is in flower or fruit; at other times keep it rather dry.
Light: Bright.
Remarks: Grow in a cold, enclosed porch or plant room. Fragrant blossoms open sporadically throughout the year.

CRASSULA ORBICULARIS
2-1-1

Description: Waxy yellow-green leaves dotted with spots; white flowers.
Size: To 14 inches. (Diameter.)
Temperature: 60–75° F.
Humidity: 20–30 per cent.
Watering: Keep soil somewhat dry.
Light: Bright.
Remarks: A low rosette plant, fine for open bubble bowls; easy to grow.

HOMALOMENA WALLISII
2-1-1

Description: Broad, oval leathery leaves, dark olive green blotched with silver.
Size: To 30 inches.
Temperature: 60–75° F.
Humidity: 30–40 per cent.
Watering: Keep soil evenly moist.
Light: Shade.
Remarks: Good bushy full plant. Propagate from stem cuttings from mature plants.

66

Codiaeum Gloriosum

Crassula orbicularis

Homalomena wallisii

Citrus taitensis

67

GARDENIA JASMINOIDES
(cape jasmine)   2-1-1

Description: Dark green leathery
leaves; double white
blooms.
Size: To 4 feet.
Temperature: 60–70° F.
Humidity: 50 per cent.
Watering: Keep soil evenly moist.
Give a deep soaking in
the sink or pail of
water once a week.
Light: Bright in summer, sun
in winter.
Remarks: Mist foliage daily to
discourage red spider.
If plant does not grow,
or is ailing, try
covering with plastic
bag held above the
foliage by stakes and
tied at the base.

CTENANTHE OPPENHEIMIANA
2-1-1

Description: Stiff white-and-green
leaves.
Size: To 36 inches.
Temperature: 55–75° F.
Humidity: 50–60 per cent.
Watering: Keep soil evenly
moist.
Light: Bright.
Remarks: Fine foliage plant but
somewhat
temperamental.

DIEFFENBACHIA AMOENA
(dumb cane)   2-1-1

Description: Heavy green-and-
white foliage.
Size: To 3 feet.
Temperature: 60–75° F.
Humidity: 20–30 per cent.
Watering: Plenty of water in
summer, but not so
much the rest of the
year.
Light: Shade.
Remarks: Best grown as tub
plant. Propagate from
stem cuttings in early
spring.

AESCHYNANTHUS SPECIOSUS
(lipstick vine)   2-1-1

Description: Spectacular orange or
red flowers.
Size: To 3 feet. (Trailing.)
Temperature: 60–75° F.
Humidity: 50–70 per cent.
Watering: Plenty of water.
Light: Somewhat shaded.
Remarks: Summer flowering; not
easy to bring into
bloom but worth the
effort. Dark glossy
leaves with a wealth of
tubular orange or red
flowers.

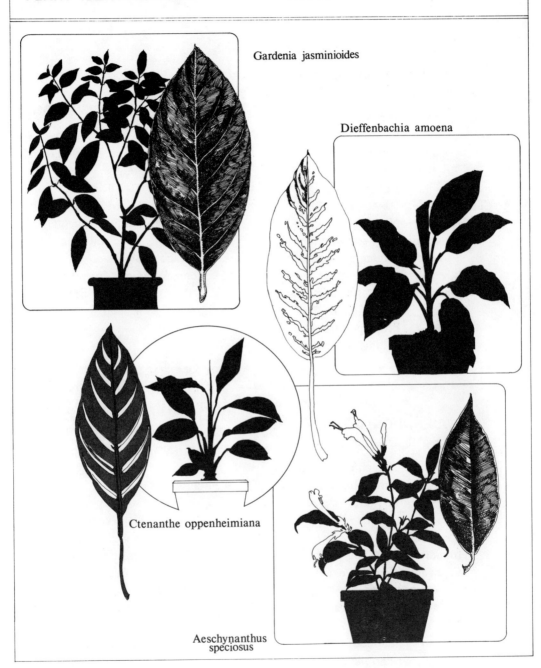

Gardenia jasminioides

Dieffenbachia amoena

Ctenanthe oppenheimiana

Aeschynanthus
speciosus

HYPOCYRTA STRIGILLOSA
(goldfish plant)　2-1-1

Description: Spreading semierect habit; reddish-orange flowers.
Size: To 24 inches. (Trailing.)
Temperature: 60–80° F.
Humidity: 60 per cent.
Watering: Keep soil evenly moist.
Light: Winter sun, summer shade.
Remarks: Set on brackets or grow in hanging baskets. Propagate from tip cuttings of new growth in spring.

PHILODENDRON WENDLANDII
(cabbage philodendron)　2-1-1

Description: 36-inch rosette; 15-inch lush green foliage.
Size: To 36 inches. (Diameter.)
Temperature: 55–75° F.
Humidity: 30–40 per cent.
Watering: Keep soil evenly moist.
Light: Shaded location.
Remarks: Excellent self-heading philodendron; good room plant.

HOFFMANNIA GHIESBREGHTII
2-1-1

Description: Exotic brown-green foliage.
Size: To 4 feet.
Temperature: 55–65° F.
Humidity: 40–50 per cent.
Watering: Keep soil evenly moist.
Light: Shade.
Remarks: Good for planters or wherever drama is needed.

CROSSANDRA INFUNDIBULIFORMIS
2-1-1

Description: Shiny, green-leaved plant; orange flowers.
Size: To 30 inches.
Temperature: 55–70° F.
Humidity: 30–40 per cent.
Watering: Keep soil evenly moist in spring; give less moisture rest of the year.
Light: Sun.
Remarks: Give an uncrowded place at the window. Flowers on and off throughout the year.

70

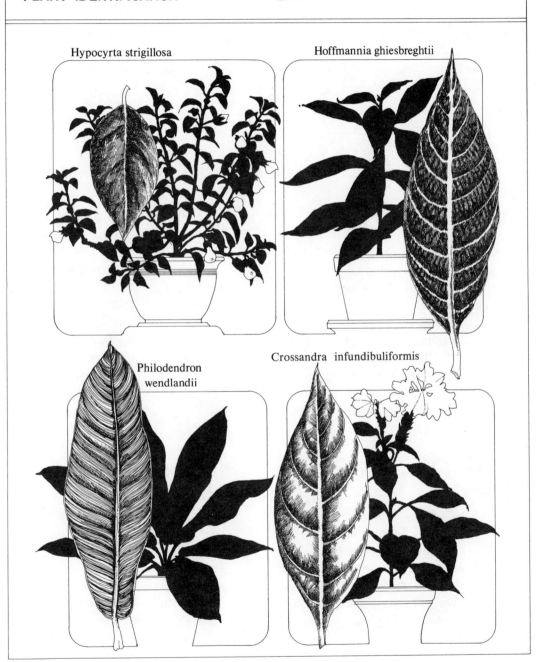

Hypocyrta strigillosa

Hoffmannia ghiesbreghtii

Philodendron wendlandii

Crossandra infundibuliformis

71

PEPEROMIA BICOLOR
2-1-2

Description: Oval, velvety metallic-
             green leaves.
Size: To 18 inches.
Temperature: 55–75° F.
Humidity: 20–30 per cent.
Watering: Keep soil evenly moist.
Light: Bright.
Remarks: Very colorful small
           plant; fine for
           terrariums.

PEPEROMIA QUANDRANGULARIS
2-1-2

Description: Small, round green
           leaves with yellow
           veins.
Size: To 10 inches.
Temperature: 55–75° F.
Humidity: 20–30 per cent.
Watering: Keep soil evenly moist.
Light: Bright.
Remarks: A low-creeping
           unusual peperomia;
           good and different.
           Fine for window sill.

PEPEROMIA VELUTINA
2-1-2

Description: Oval, velvety bronzy-
           green leaves.
Size: To 14 inches.
Temperature: 55–75° F.
Humidity: 20–30 per cent.
Watering: Keep soil evenly moist.
Light: Bright.
Remarks: Very colorful small
           plant.

PEPEROMIA ACUMINATA
2-1-2

Description: Waxy green leaves
           with curved tip.
Size: To 16 inches.
Temperature: 55–75° F.
Humidity: 30–40 per cent.
Watering: Keep soil evenly moist.
Light: Bright.
Remarks: Excellent terrarium
           plant.

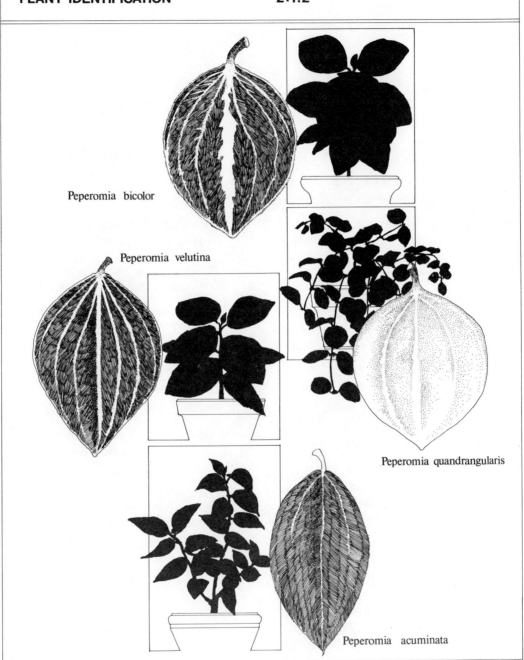

Peperomia bicolor

Peperomia velutina

Peperomia quandrangularis

Peperomia acuminata

CYANOTIS KEWENSIS
(pussy ears)   2-1-3

Description: Succulent creeper, with hairy velvety brown foliage.
Size: To 10 inches.
Temperature: 55–70° F.
Humidity: 20–30 per cent.
Watering: Keep soil evenly moist.
Light: Bright.
Remarks: Desirable for its purple blooms in spring.

DRACAENA SANDERIANA
(corn plant)   2-1-3

Description: 9-inch green leaves banded white.
Size: To 5 feet.
Temperature: 55–75° F.
Humidity: 20–30 per cent.
Watering: Keep soil evenly moist. Do not let water accumulate on leaves.
Light: Bright, but no sun.
Remarks: Survives under untoward conditions.

SEDUM ADOLPHII
(stonecrop)   2-1-3

Description: Yellow-green bush type; white flowers in spring.
Size: To 6 inches.
Temperature: 50–70° F.
Humidity: 20–30 per cent.
Watering: Dry soil out between waterings.
Light: Sun.
Remarks: Excellent for dish gardens.

SANSEVIERIA HAHNI
(snake plant)   2-1-3

Description: Vaselike rosette of broad leaves, dark green and pale green crossbanded.
Size: To 20 inches.
Temperature: 55–75° F.
Humidity: 20–30 per cent.
Watering: Water; allow to dry out before watering again.
Light: Shade.
Remarks: One of the low-growing Sansevierias for dish gardens.

74

Cyanotis kewensis

Sedum adolphi

Dracaena sanderiana

Sansevieria hahni

ASPIDISTRA ELATIOR
VARIEGATA
(cast-iron plant)   2-1-3

Description: Green-and-white-
striped foliage.
Size: To 24 inches.
Temperature: 50–70° F.
Humidity: 20–30 per cent.
Watering: Keep soil evenly moist.
Light: Bright.
Remarks: Foliage is sometimes
complemented by
sprays of purple-brown
flowers. Good plant for
north windows. Grow
several plants to a pot
for a good display.

DRACAENA FRAGRANS
MASSANGEANA
(corn plant)   2-1-3

Description: Arching yellow-and-
green 24-inch leaves.
Size: To 5 feet.
Temperature: 55–75° F.
Humidity: 20–30 per cent.
Watering: Keep soil evenly moist.
Light: Bright, but no sun.
Remarks: Can be trained to grow
like a small tree.
Propagate from stem
cuttings.

ASPIDISTRA ELATIOR
(cast-iron plant)   2-1-3

Description: Shiny green-black
leaves.
Size: To 24 inches.
Temperature: 50–70° F.
Humidity: 20–30 per cent.
Watering: Keep soil evenly moist.
Light: Shade.
Remarks: Fine green accent for
orphan north windows
and survives almost
any situation. Divide
crowns for new plants.

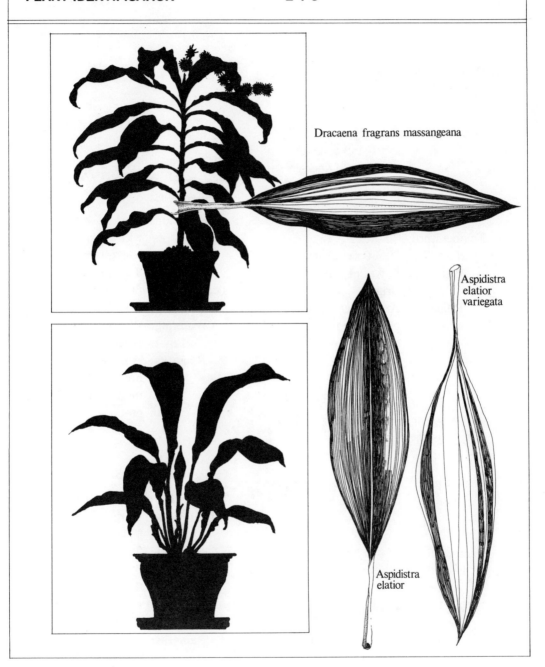

Dracaena fragrans massangeana

Aspidistra elatior variegata

Aspidistra elatior

CALATHEA PICTURATA ARGENTEA
2-2-1

Description: Small plants with short-stalked leaves, silvery with dark green borders, wine-red beneath.
Size: To 16 inches.
Temperature: 70–80° F.
Humidity: 70–80 per cent.
Watering: Plenty of water.
Light: Bright.
Remarks: An exotic-appearing plant, fine for terrariums or table accent.

APHELANDRA SQUARROSA LOUISAE
2-2-1

Description: Compact, with shiny corrugated leaves, shaded yellow bracts.
Size: To 20 inches.
Temperature: 55–75° F.
Humidity: 20–30 per cent.
Watering: Plenty of water.
Light: Bright.
Remarks: Long-lasting terminal clusters of spring or summer flowers.

CALATHEA ZEBRINA
(zebra plant)   2-2-1

Description: Dark velvety leaves with chartreuse background.
Size: To 36 inches.
Temperature: 60–80° F.
Humidity: To 80 per cent.
Watering: Plenty of water.
Light: Bright.
Remarks: A delightful houseplant; does better indoors than others in group.

CALATHEA ROSEO-PICTA
2-2-1

Description: Dark-green-and-red leaves.
Size: To 12 inches.
Temperature: 60–80° F.
Humidity: To 80 per cent.
Watering: Plenty of water.
Light: Bright.
Remarks: Fine foliage plant from Brazil.

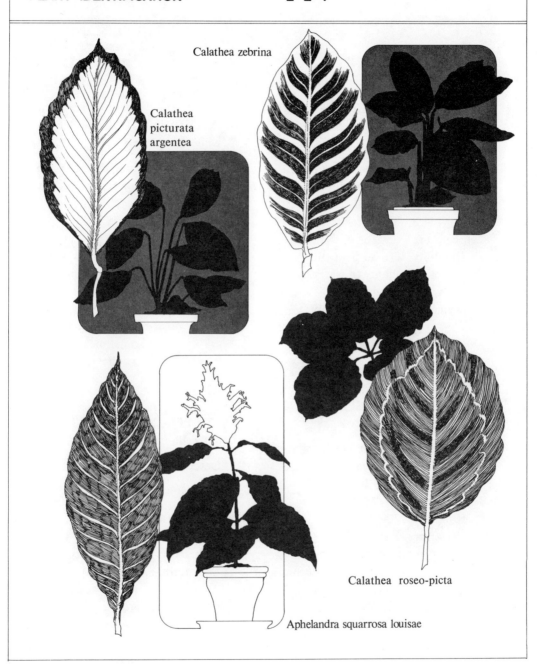

Calathea zebrina

Calathea
picturata
argentea

Calathea roseo-picta

Aphelandra squarrosa louisae

APHELANDRA CHAMISSONIANA
(zebra plant) 2-2-1

Description: Dramatic oval leaves
with heavy veining,
terminal clusters of
cheerful yellow bracts.
Size: To 14 inches.
Temperature: 55–75° F.
Humidity: 20–30 per cent.
Watering: Plenty of water.
Light: Bright.
Remarks: A popular plant; good
gift item and ideal for
table decoration.

SPATHIPHYLLUM CLEVELANDII
(white flag plant) 2-2-1

Description: Long leaves; white
flowers.
Size: To 20 inches.
Temperature: 55–75° F.
Humidity: 20–30 per cent.
Watering: Keep soil evenly moist
except in winter.
Light: Bright.
Remarks: Bloom usually appears
in winter, but
sometimes in summer
or fall.

DIEFFENBACHIA SPLENDENS
(dumbcane) 2-2-1

Description: Velvety green foliage
with small white dots.
Size: To 3 feet.
Temperature: 60–75° F.
Humidity: 20–30 per cent.
Watering: Plenty of water in
summer, but not so
much the rest of the
year.
Light: Shade.
Remarks: Graceful plant, with
large ornamental
leaves.

SCHEFFLERA DIGITATA
(umbrella plant) 2-2-1

Description: Yellow hairy foliage, 7
to 10 leaflets; greenish-
yellow flowers.
Size: To 60 inches.
Temperature: 55–75° F.
Humidity: 20–30 per cent.
Watering: Water only once or
twice a week.
Light: Bright.
Remarks: A tough tub plant that
survives untoward
conditions.

Aphelandra chamissoniana

Spathiphyllum Clevelandii

Dieffenbachia splendens

Schefflera digitata

ACHIMENES GRANDIFLORA
(rainbow plant)   2-5-1

Description: Oval-toothed leaves; red-purple flowers.
Size: To 16 inches.
Temperature: 75–85° F.
Humidity: 50–70 per cent.
Watering: Water thoroughly, then allow to dry before watering again.
Light: Sun.
Remarks: Grows from tuber; pot in spring for summer bloom, or in fall for winter.

AUCUBA CRANDIFOLIA
(gold-dust tree)   2-5-1

Description: Leathery dark green leaves blotched with yellow.
Size: 26–48 inches.
Temperature: 60–75° F.
Humidity: 20–30 per cent.
Watering: Keep soil somewhat dry.
Light: Bright or shade.
Remarks: A good low-growing lush plant; excellent accent.

AUCUBA LONGIFOLIA
2-5-1

Description: Deep green leaves with white or yellow blotches.
Size: 26–48 inches.
Temperature: 60–75° F.
Humidity: 20–30 per cent.
Watering: Keep soil somewhat dry.
Light: Bright or shade.
Remarks: Good accent plant.

ACHIMENES LONGIFLORA
(rainbow plant)   2-5-1

Description: Oval leaves; long-tubed violet-blue flowers.
Size: To 2 feet.
Temperature: 75–85° F.
Humidity: 50–70 per cent.
Watering: Water thoroughly, then allow to dry before watering again.
Light: Sun.
Remarks: Blooms in spring and summer. Grows from tubers.

Achimenes grandiflora

Aucuba longifolia

Aucuba grandifolia

Achimenes longiflora

AESCHYNANTHUS PULCHRUM
(lipstick vine)   3-1-1

Description: Red-and-yellow
flowers.
Size: To 3 feet. (Trailing.)
Temperature: 60–75° F.
Humidity: Spray frequently to
keep humidity high,
from 50 to 70 per cent.
Watering: Plenty of water.
Light: Somewhat shaded
position.
Remarks: Summer flowering; not
easy to bring to bloom,
but worth while. New
plants from stem or tip
cuttings.

CALATHEA CONCINNA
3-1-1

Description: Dark green feather
design running into
deeper green and
purple underneath.
Size: To 20 inches.
Temperature: 60–80° F.
Humidity: To 80 per cent.
Watering: Plenty of water.
Light: Bright.
Remarks: Outstanding foliage;
propagate by dividing
plants in spring.

HOYA MOTOSKEI
(wax plant)   3-1-1

Description: Oval leaves with silver
spots; pink blooms.
Size: To 4 feet. (Trailing.)
Temperature: 55–75° F.
Humidity: 40–50 per cent.
Watering: Plenty of water in
spring, summer, and
fall. Keep somewhat
dry in winter.
Light: Sun.
Remarks: Best grown on a trellis
or support, but can also
be handsome in a
hanging basket.

CLERODENDRUM THOMSONAE
(glory bower)   3-1-1

Description: Lush green foliage,
with white-and-deep
crimson flowers in
spring.
Size: To 6 feet.
Temperature: 50–65° F.
Humidity: 30–40 per cent.
Watering: Keep soil evenly moist
except in winter.
Light: Sun.
Remarks: Decorative as pot
plant or in baskets.
Lots of color for little
effort.

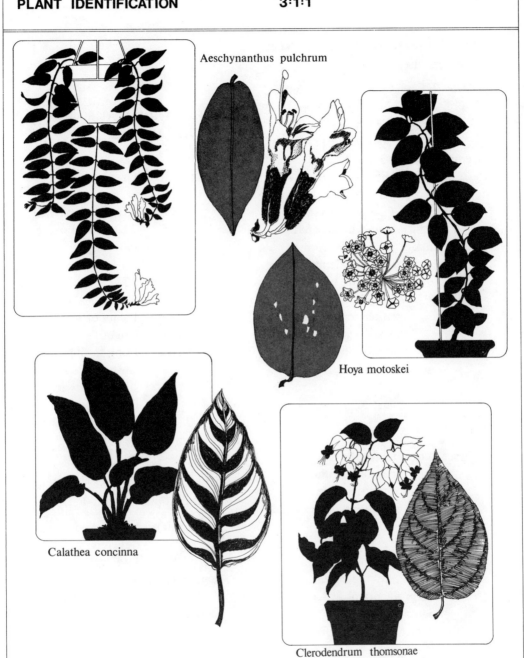

Aeschynanthus pulchrum

Hoya motoskei

Calathea concinna

Clerodendrum thomsonae

AESCHYNANTHUS LOBBIANUS
(lipstick vine)   3-1-1

Description: Clusters of brilliant red flowers at the tips of branches.
Size: To 3 feet. (Trailing.)
Temperature: 60–75° F.
Humidity: High, from 50 to 70 per cent.
Watering: Plenty of water.
Light: Somewhat shaded.
Remarks: Summer flowering; rather difficult to bring to bloom, but worth the effort. Trailing epiphytes, with dark glossy leaves and tubular flowers.

CALATHEA VEITCHIANA
3-1-1

Description: Leaves have a peacock-feather design: brown, chartreuse, green, and red.
Size: To 30 inches.
Temperature: 60–80° F.
Humidity: To 80 per cent.
Watering: Plenty of water.
Light: Bright.
Remarks: Very colorful. Fine small table or desk plant.

APHELANDRA AURANTICA ROEZLII
3-1-1

Description: Gray-green or dark green leaves attractively veined white; vivid orange-red blooms.
Size: To 16 inches.
Temperature: 55–75° F.
Humidity: 20–30 per cent.
Watering: Plenty of water.
Light: Bright.
Remarks: Long-lasting terminal clusters of spring or summer flowers. Propagate from tip cuttings in spring.

DRACAENA GODSEFFIANA
(gold-dust plant)   3-1-1

Description: Yellow-and-green 6-inch leaves.
Size: To 5 feet.
Temperature: 55–75° F.
Humidity: 20–30 per cent.
Watering: Keep soil evenly moist.
Light: Bright, but no sun.
Remarks: Plant survives untoward conditions.

Aeschynanthus lobbianus

Aphelandra aurantica roezlii

Dracaena godseffiana

Calathea veitchiana

AGLAONEMA ROBELINII
(Chinese evergreen)   3-1-1

Description: Blue-green leaves; white flowers. Very robust.
Size: To 3 feet.
Temperature: 60–75° F.
Humidity: 20–30 per cent.
Watering: Keep soil evenly moist.
Light: Bright or shade.
Remarks: Can thrive under most circumstances.

MEDINILLA MAGNIFICA
(glory bower)   3-1-1

Description: Lush blue-green plant; pendulous panicles of carmine flowers in pink bracts.
Size: To 40 inches.
Temperature: 55–75° F.
Humidity: 70 per cent.
Watering: Keep soil evenly moist. Dry out somewhat in winter.
Light: Bright.
Remarks: Blossoming can occur any time of year, but only in mature plant in 8- or 10-inch tub.

HOYA BELLA
(wax plant)   3-1-1

Description: Tiny leaves; umbels of purple-centered white blooms.
Size: To 20 inches. (Trailing or Vining.)
Temperature: 55–75° F.
Humidity: 30–40 per cent.
Watering: Plenty of water in spring, summer, and fall; in winter let go almost dry.
Light: Sun.
Remarks: Do not remove stem or spur on which flowers have been produced because this is the source of next season's bloom.

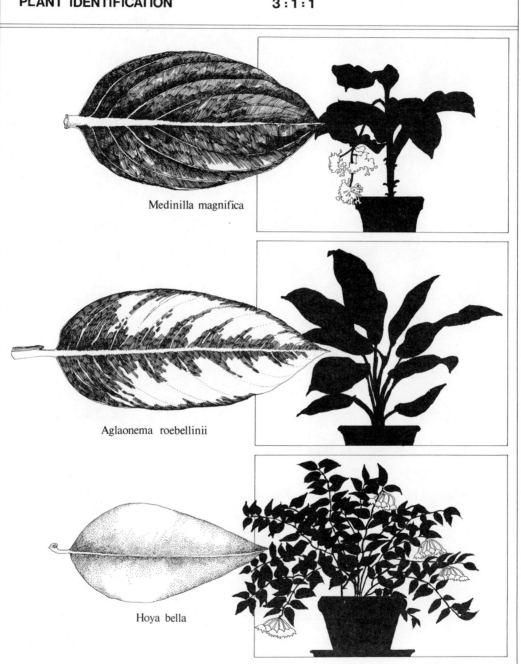

Medinilla magnifica

Aglaonema roebellinii

Hoya bella

TRADESCANTIA ALBIFLORA
(wandering Jew)   3-1-3

Description: Fleshy, lance-shaped
bluish-green leaves.
Size: To 36 inches.
(Vining.)
Temperature: 55–75° F.
Humidity: 20–30 per cent.
Watering: Keep moist.
Light: Bright or shade.
Remarks: Good all-around
houseplant. New
plants from cuttings.

DRACAENA GOLDIEANA
3-1-3

Description: Large bright green
leaves splashed with
yellow markings.
Size: To 36 inches.
Temperature: 55–75° F.
Humidity: 20–30 per cent.
Watering: Water, allow to dry
before watering again.
Light: Bright.
Remarks: Somewhat less
impressive than others
in the family but still a
good houseplant.

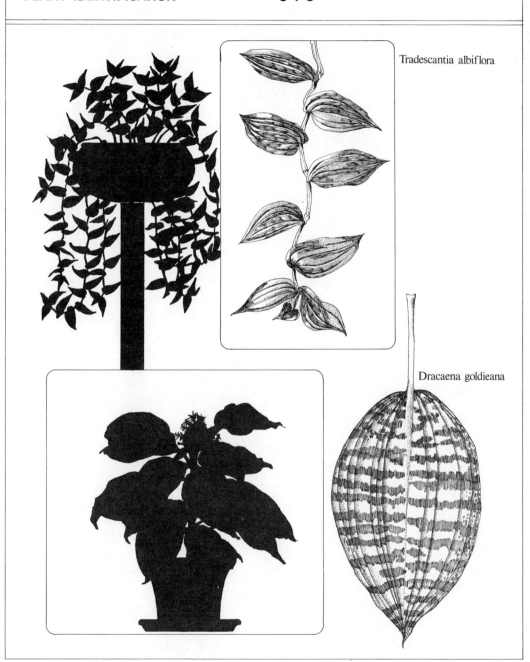

Tradescantia albiflora

Dracaena goldieana

ZEBRINA PENDULA
(wandering Jew)   3-1-3

Description: Purple leaves with
silver bands; trailing
habit.
Size: To 48 inches.
(Vining.)
Temperature: 55–75° F.
Humidity: 30–40 per cent.
Watering: Keep soil evenly moist,
or grow in plain water.
Light: Bright.
Remarks: A fast-growing popular
hanging plant; new
varieties available.
New plants from
cuttings any time.

SANSEVIERIA 'SILVER HAHNI'
(snake plant)   3-1-3

Description: Metallic, pale silvery-
green leaves.
Size: To 26 inches.
Temperature: 55–75° F.
Humidity: 20–30 per cent.
Watering: Water; allow to dry
before watering again.
Light: Shade.
Remarks: Easy-to-grow colorful
plant; for planters or
dish gardens.

Zebrina pendula

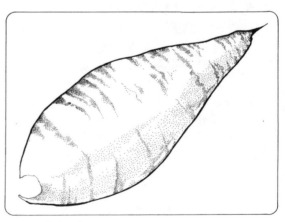

Sansevieria silver hahni

93

CALATHEA LEOPARDINA
3-2-1

Description: Waxy green foliage with contrasting darker green.
Size: To 12 inches.
Temperature: 60–80° F.
Humidity: To 80 per cent.
Watering: Plenty of water.
Light: Bright.
Remarks: Not easy to grow, but worthwhile because of its beautiful foliage.

DIEFFENBACHIA HOFFMANNII
3-2-1

Description: Oblong, pointed, satiny green leaves; marked white.
Size: To 48 inches.
Temperature: 55–75° F.
Humidity: 20–40 per cent.
Watering: Water; allow to dry before watering again.
Light: Bright.
Remarks: Good room plant; dislikes drafts.

AGLAONEMA COMMUTATUM
(Chinese evergreen)   3-2-1

Description: Silver markings on dark green leaves.
Size: To 2 feet.
Temperature: 60–75° F.
Humidity: 20–30 per cent.
Watering: Keep soil evenly moist.
Light: Shade.
Remarks: Thrives under untoward conditions. Only pot-bound plant will bloom, but bloom it does, luxuriantly in late summer and early fall.

AGLAONEMA PICTUM
(Chinese evergreen)   3-2-1

Description: Dark green velvety leaves, silver spotted.
Size: Dwarf to 1 foot.
Temperature: 60–75° F.
Humidity: 20–30 per cent.
Watering: Keep soil evenly moist.
Light: Bright or shade.
Remarks: From tropical forests, it thrives under untoward conditions. Only pot-bound plant will bloom.

Calathea leopardina

Dieffenbachia hoffmannii

Aglaonema commutatum

Aglaonema pictum

RIVINA HUMILIS
(rouge plant)   3-2-1

Description: Oval leaves, drooping
clusters of white
flowers, and lustrous
red berries on and off
throughout the year.
Size: To 24 inches.
Temperature: 55–70° F.
Humidity: 30–40 per cent.
Watering: Keep soil evenly moist.
Light: Sun.
Remarks: Very pretty at the
window. New plants
from cuttings.

AGLAONEMA SIMPLEX
(Chinese evergreen)   3-2-1

Description: Grows like a weed in a
jar of water.
Size: To 3 feet.
Temperature: 60–75° F.
Humidity: 20–30 per cent.
Watering: Keep soil evenly moist.
Light: Shade.
Remarks: Hardy grower.

DATURA MOLLIS
(angel's-trumpet)   3-2-1

Description: Large dark green
leaves, nodding
salmon-pink flowers.
Size: To 5 feet.
Temperature: 55–65° F.
Humidity: 50 per cent.
Watering: Let soil dry out
somewhat between
waterings.
Light: Bright sun.
Remarks: Because of its
mammoth flowers, this
plant is desirable
indoors if you have
space for it.

RUELLIA AMOENA
3-2-1

Description: Waxy oval leaves; red
flowers.
Size: To 24 inches.
Temperature: 60–75° F.
Humidity: 30–40 per cent.
Watering: Keep soil barely moist.
Light: Sun.
Remarks: Good for basket or
bracket; dependable
and colorful in the
window garden.

Rivina humilis

Datura mollis

Aglaonema simplex

Ruellia amoena

ACHIMENES PATENS
(rainbow plant)   3-4-1

Description: Ovate pointed leaves;
           violet-blue flowers.
Size: To 1½ feet.
Temperature: 75–85° F.
Humidity: 50–70 per cent.
Watering: Keep moist, then allow
         to dry before watering
         again.
Light: Sun.
Remarks: Showy flowers.

ACALYPHA WILKESIANA
  MACROPHYLLA
3-4-1

Description: Bronze-and-copper
           foliage; red blooms.
Size: To 30 inches.
Temperature: 65–75° F.
Humidity: Around 50 per cent.
Watering: Keep soil evenly moist.
Light: Sun.
Remarks: For a good show, put
         several plants in one
         container.

ACALYPHA GODSEFFIANA
(chenille-plant)   3-4-1

Description: Bright green, yellow-
           edged leaves; green-
           white flowers.
Size: To 20 inches.
Temperature: 65–75° F.
Humidity: Around 50 per cent.
Watering: Keep soil evenly moist.
Light: Sun.
Remarks: For a good show, put
         several plants in one
         container.

LANTANA CAMARA
3-4-1

Description: Orange summer
           flowers; hairy leaves.
Size: To 20 inches.
Temperature: 50–70° F.
Humidity: 30–40 per cent.
Watering: Plenty of water in
         summer; let get
         somewhat dry in
         winter.
Light: Sun.
Remarks: Temperamental to grow
         but good color.

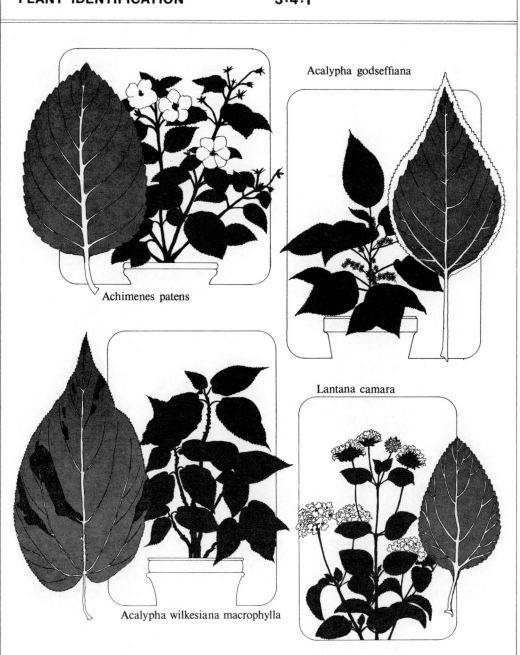

Acalypha godseffiana

Achimenes patens

Lantana camara

Acalypha wilkesiana macrophylla

FUCHSIA HYBRID
(Lady's-eardrops)   3-4-1

Description: Dark green leaves;
stellar pendent flowers.
Size: To 60 inches.
(Trailing.)
Temperature: 55–75° F.
Humidity: 20–40 per cent.
Watering: Keep soil evenly moist.
Light: Bright.
Remarks: Hundreds of varieties.
Some fuchsias do well
indoors; most need
outdoor summering.

CAMELLIA JAPONICA
3-4-1

Description: Produces leathery dark
green leaves and large
flowers in a wide range
of whites, pinks, and
reds.
Size: To 48 inches.
Temperature: 45–60° F.
Humidity: 60 per cent.
Watering: Never let soil dry out,
and mist foliage every
day in summer, about
every other day the rest
of the year.
Light: Bright.
Remarks: Ideal as floor plant in
front of cool window or
for sun porch or plant
room.

KOHLERIA ERIANTHA
3-4-1

Description: Erect grower, with
bright red flowers from
summer to fall.
Size: To 24 inches.
Temperature: 60–70° F.
Humidity: 60 per cent, but do not
mist plant.
Watering: Heavily in growth,
much less the rest of
the time. Never allow
plants to become
completely dry.
Light: Bright.
Remarks: Fine upright grower,
with colorful tubular
flowers and attractive
foliage.

OSMANTHUS FRAGRANS
(sweet olive)   3-4-1

Description: Plain green leaves;
heavily scented tiny
white flowers on and
off throughout the
year.
Size: To 24 inches.
Temperature: 60–70° F.
Humidity: 40–50 per cent.
Watering: Keep soil evenly moist.
Light: Sun.
Remarks: Excellent houseplant
and valued for indoor
fragrance.

Fuchsia hybrid

Kohleria eriantha

Camellia japonica

Osmanthus fragrans

BEGONIA BOWERI
(eyelash begonia)   3-4-2

Description: Small, with vivid green
leaves with brown
patches and hairs on
leaf edges.
Size: To 14 inches.
Temperature: 60–75° F.
Humidity: 20–40 per cent.
Watering: Keep soil evenly moist.
Light: Bright.
Remarks: An excellent small
begonia for window or
terrarium growing.
Propagate from
cuttings or sow seed.

BEGONIA METALLICA
3-4-2

Description: Pointed metallic green
leaves; pink flowers.
Size: To 38 inches.
Temperature: 60–75° F.
Humidity: 20–40 per cent.
Watering: Keep soil evenly moist.
Light: Bright.
Remarks: Good window-sill
plant.

BEGONIA EVANSIANA
(hardy begonia)   3-4-2

Description: Olive-green oval
leaves; pink flowers.
Size: To 60 inches.
(Trailing.)
Temperature: 45–70° F.
Humidity: 20–40 per cent.
Watering: Plenty of water.
Light: Bright.
Remarks: Can take some frost;
robust plant.

BEGONIA IMPERIALIS
3-4-2

Description: Small, heart-shaped,
velvety green leaves.
Size: To 40 inches.
(Trailing.)
Temperature: 55–75° F.
Humidity: 20–40 per cent.
Watering: Water; allow to dry out
before watering again.
Light: Bright.
Remarks: Makes full and bushy,
somewhat trailing,
plant; good for
windows.

Begonia boweri

Begonia evansiana

Begonia metallica

Begonia imperialis

MALPIGHIA COCCIGERA
(miniature holly)   3-5-1

Description: Small glossy leaves,
crepelike in texture;
pink flowers.
Size: To 28 inches.
Temperature: 60–75° F.
Humidity: 30–50 per cent.
Watering: Keep soil evenly moist.
Light: Bright.
Remarks: It does look like
miniature holly and
makes a fine indoor
plant.

GYNURA AURANTIACA
(velvet plant)   3-5-1

Description: Large purple leaves.
Size: To 30 inches.
(Trailing.)
Temperature: 65–75° F.
Humidity: 40–60 per cent.
Watering: Keep soil evenly moist.
Light: Bright.
Remarks: Desirable for planter
boxes or where special
accent is needed.
Propagate by cuttings.

HIBISCUS ROSA-SINENSIS
(hibiscus)   3-5-1

Description: Large serrate dark
green leaves; big pink
flowers.
Size: Branching to 5 feet.
Temperature: 55–75° F.
Humidity: 20–40 per cent.
Watering: Keep soil very moist.
Light: Sun.
Remarks: Excellent room plants,
and they do bloom
indoors.

Gynura aurantiaca

Malpighia coccigera

Hibiscus rosa-sinensis

EPISCIA CUPREATA
(peacock plant) 3-6-1

Description: Copper foliage dusted
with white hairs;
scarlet flowers.
Size: To 20 inches.
(Trailing.)
Temperature: 65–80° F.
Humidity: 50 per cent.
Watering: Plenty of water all
year.
Light: Bright.
Remarks: Exotic foliage and
brilliant flowers in
spring and summer.

KOHLERIA AMABILIS
3-6-1

Description: Green leaves; pink
blooms in spring and
summer.
Size: To 16 inches.
Temperature: 60–80° F.
Humidity: 60 per cent.
Watering: Water heavily in
growth, much less the
rest of the time (only
about once a week),
but never allow plants
to become completely
dry. Use room-
temperature water.
Light: Bright.
Remarks: Good basket plant.
Separate large
rhizomes for new
plants.

IMPATIENS HOLSTII
(patience plant) 3-6-1

Description: Reddish leaves; red
flowers.
Size: To 24 inches.
Temperature: 50–65° F.
Humidity: 20–30 per cent.
Watering: Keep soil evenly moist
in summer, barely
moist in winter.
Light: Bright.
Remarks: Excellent window
plant that offers color
almost all year.

KOHLERIA LINDENIANA
3-6-1

Description: Erect, with fragrant
violet-and-white
flowers in late fall.
Size: To 10 inches.
Temperature: 60–80° F.
Humidity: 60 per cent, but do not
mist.
Watering: Water heavily during
growth, much less the
rest of the time. Never
allow to become
completely dry.
Light: Bright.
Remarks: Upright grower, with
colorful tubular
flowers.

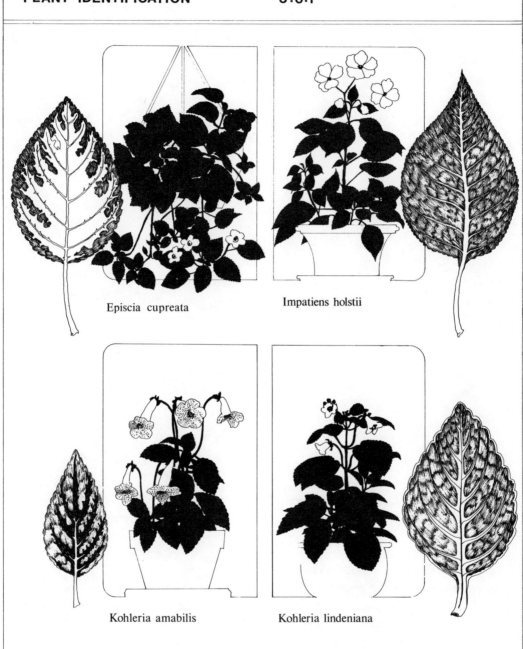

Episcia cupreata

Impatiens holstii

Kohleria amabilis

Kohleria lindeniana

SAINTPAULIA IONANTHA
(African violet)   3-6-1

Description: Dark coppery green leaves.
Size: To 20 inches.
Temperature: 55–75° F.
Humidity: 20–30 per cent.
Watering: Keep evenly moist.
Light: Bright.
Remarks: Used with *S. confusa* to propagate many violet hybrids.

COLEUS BLUMEI
(painted-leaf plant)   3-6-1

Description: Colorful plant with bright plumage of plum, red, pink, green, or yellow.
Size: To 16 inches.
Temperature: 55–65° F.
Humidity: 20–30 per cent.
Watering: Needs plenty of water.
Light: Bright.
Remarks: Put outside in summer for blue flowers.

Saintpaulia ionantha

Coleus blumei

SAINTPAULIA 'VIKING'
(African violet)   3-6-1

Description: Large white-flowered variety.
Size: To 18 inches.
Temperature: 55–75° F.
Humidity: 20–30 per cent.
Watering: Keep moist.
Light: Bright.
Remarks: Another good violet.

SAINTPAULIA 'ORCHID BEAUTY'
(African violet)   3-6-1

Description: Fine, large orchid-colored flowers.
Size: To 20 inches.
Temperature: 55–75° F.
Humidity: 20–30 per cent.
Watering: Keep moist.
Light: Bright.
Remarks: Good flowering variety. Propagate from leaf cuttings.

SAINTPAULIA 'RAFFIA'
(African violet)   3-6-1

Description: Fine floriferous violet.
Size: To 20 inches.
Temperature: 55–75° F.
Humidity: 20–30 per cent.
Watering: Keep moist.
Light: Bright.
Remarks: Good flowering type.

Saintpaulia Viking

Saintpaulia Orchid Beauty

Saintpaulia Raffia

PILEA REPENS
3-6-2

Description:	Tiny, quilted, coppery-brown round leaves.
Size:	To 10 inches.
Temperature:	60–75° F.
Humidity:	30–40 per cent.
Watering:	Likes plenty of water.
Light:	Bright.
Remarks:	An excellent terrarium or dish-garden plant.

PLECTRANTHUS OERTENDAHII
(Swedish ivy)   3-6-2

Description:	Broad bronzy-green leaves with silver veins.
Size:	To 40 inches. (Trailing.)
Temperature:	55–75° F.
Humidity:	20–30 per cent.
Watering:	Keep evenly moist.
Light:	Bright.
Remarks:	Good basket plant that can take abuse; several species available. New plants from cuttings any time.

112

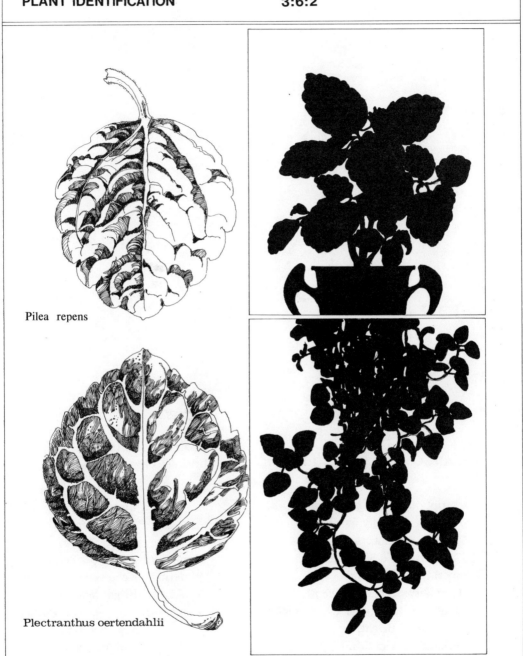

Pilea repens

Plectranthus oertendahlii

PELARGONIUM 'GRAND SLAM'
4-4-2

Description: Dark green leaves,
lovely flame-red
flowers.
Size: To 30 inches.
Temperature: 50–70° F.
Humidity: 20–30 per cent.
Watering: Keep soil evenly moist.
Light: Bright.
Remarks: Good full-blooming
bushy geranium.

BEGONIA CHEIMANTHA
(Christmas begonia)   4-4-2

Description: Stiff waxy foliage; fine
winter flowers.
Size: To 30 inches.
Temperature: 55–75° F.
Humidity: 20–30 per cent.
Watering: Keep soil evenly moist.
Light: Bright light; no sun.
Remarks: Many varieties with
large handsome
flowers; some
temperamental.

114

Pelargonium Grand Slam

Begonia cheimantha

BEGONIA ERYTHROPHYLLA
(beefsteak begonia)   4-4-2

Description: Fleshy green round leaves; pink flowers.
Size: To 30 inches.
Temperature: 58–65° F.
Humidity: 30–40 per cent.
Watering: Water thoroughly; allow to dry before watering again.
Light: Bright.
Remarks: Makes a full bushy plant; mature specimen handsome. Good window or hanging plant.

BEGONIA KELLERMANNII
(penny begonia)   4-4-2

Description: Cupped, oval yellow-green leaves; pink flowers.
Size: To 30 inches.
Temperature: 55–75° F.
Humidity: 20–40 per cent.
Watering: Keep soil evenly moist.
Light: Bright.
Remarks: Good begonia. Bushy and always attractive; slightly temperamental.

BEGONIA MAZAE
4-4-2

Description: Round satiny leaves blotched in various greens.
Size: To 30 inches.
Temperature: 60–75° F.
Humidity: 20–40 per cent.
Watering: Keep soil somewhat dry.
Light: Bright.
Remarks: A good small begonia with dense blooms.

BEGONIA PAULENSIS
4-4-2

Description: Large and hairy quilted green leaves with pale veins.
Size: To 40 inches.
Temperature: 60–75° F.
Humidity: 30–40 per cent.
Watering: Keep soil evenly moist.
Light: Bright.
Remarks: A tough rhizomatous begonia that takes abuse.

116

Begonia
erythrophylla

Begonia
kellermanni

Begonia
mazae

Begonia
paulensis

EUPHORBIA SPLENDENS
(crown-of-thorns)   5-1-1

Description: Tiny green leaves; red
blooms.
Size: To 24 inches.
(Branching.)
Temperature: 50–75° F.
Humidity: 20–30 per cent.
Watering: Keep soil evenly moist
but never soggy.
Light: Sun.
Remarks: A spiny branching
climber well worth
indoor space. Depend-
able to bloom.

JATROPHA PANDURIFOLIA
5-1-1

Description: Oval, fiddle-shaped
leaves, somewhat
toothed; fine red
flowers.
Size: Branching to 4 feet.
Temperature: 60–75° F.
Humidity: 30–40 per cent.
Watering: Keep soil evenly moist.
Light: Sun.
Remarks: Good bushy plant;
cut back somewhat if
it gets straggly.

IXORA CHINENSIS
(flame-of-the-woods)   5-1-1

Description: Red to white blooms
with ornamental
foliage; 4-inch leaves.
Size: Growth to 36 inches.
Temperature: 50–70° F.
Humidity: 40–50 per cent.
Watering: Keep soil evenly moist.
Light: Sun.
Remarks: Even young plant
blooms; a worthwhile
plant.

MURRAEA EXOTICA
(orange jessamine)   5-1-1

Description: Evergreen shrub with
glossy green ferny
foliage; very fragrant
clusters of white
flowers in summer.
Size: To 26 inches.
Temperature: 55–70° F.
Humidity: 30–40 per cent.
Watering: Plenty of water, less in
winter.
Light: Sun.
Remarks: Smells like orange
blossoms; lovely
scented plant for
indoors. Propagate
from cuttings.

118

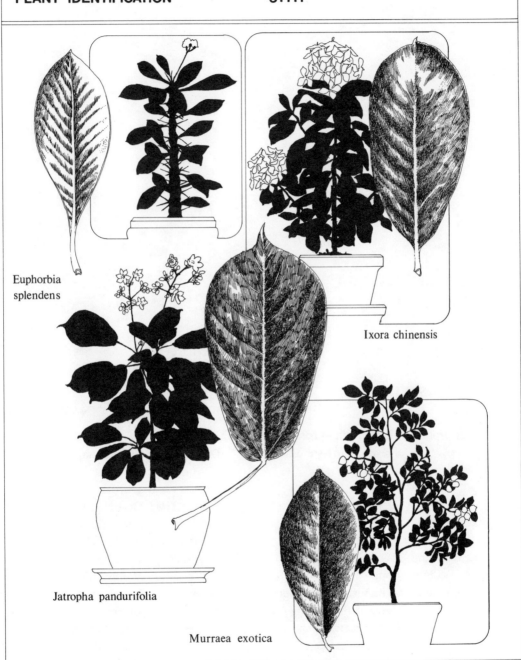

Euphorbia
splendens

Ixora chinensis

Jatropha pandurifolia

Murraea exotica

119

AGAVE STRIATA
6-1-1

Description: Angled gray-green leaves; short-stemmed rosette.

Size: To 12 inches. (Diameter.)

Temperature: 55–75° F.

Humidity: 30–40 per cent.

Watering: Keep somewhat dry.

Light: Sun.

Remarks: A handsome succulent well worth growing for its symmetrical shape. New plants from offshoots at base.

DRACAENA MARGINATA
(decorator plant)   6-1-1

Description: Sword-shaped dark green, red-edged leaves.

Size: Branching to 6 feet. (Branching).

Temperature: 55–75° F.

Humidity: 20–30 per cent.

Watering: Water; allow to dry before watering again.

Light: Bright; no sun.

Remarks: One of the finest room plants. Grows years with little care.

120

Agave striata

Dracaena marginata

CYMBIDIUM 'DOS PUEBLOS'
6-1-3

Description: Grasslike tapering green leaves.
Size: To 60 inches.
Temperature: 55–75° F.
Humidity: 30–40 per cent.
Watering: Keep soil moist except after flowering; let rest a few weeks.
Light: Bright; some sun.
Remarks: Needs cooling period (45° F.) to flower. New plants by dividing mature ones.

COELOGYNE CRISTATA
(white crystal orchid)   6-1-3

Description: Papery leaves and 3-inch crystal-white flowers in January and February.
Size: To 20 inches.
Temperature: 50–60° F.
Humidity: 40 to 60 per cent.
Watering: Keep evenly moist but reduce watering before and after blooming.
Light: Bright.
Remarks: This cool-growing epiphytic orchid performs better at home than in the greenhouse. Needs a rest period.

CHLOROPHYTUM COMOSUM VARIEGATUM
(spider plant)   6-1-3

Description: Green leaves with white margins.
Size: To 60 inches. (Trailing.)
Temperature: 50–75° F.
Humidity: 20–30 per cent.
Watering: Let soil dry out between waterings.
Light: Bright.
Remarks: Excellent for baskets. Runners on offsets root quickly in water for new plants.

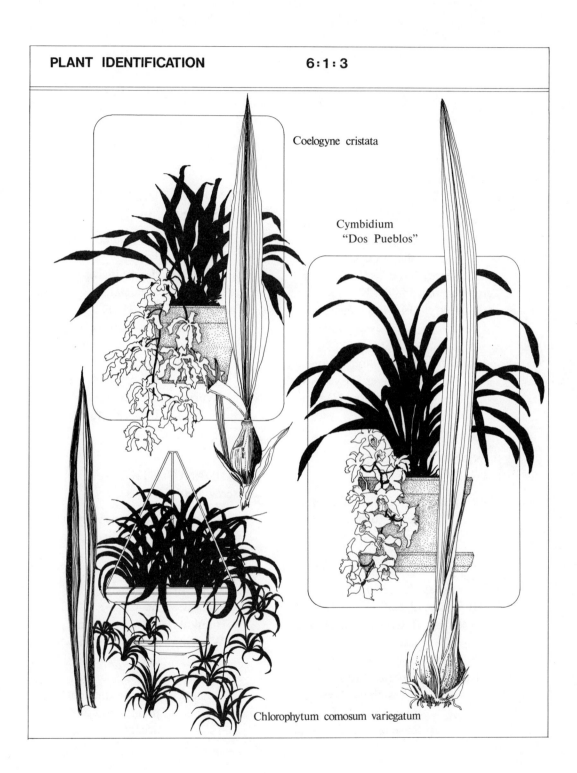

Coelogyne cristata

Cymbidium
"Dos Pueblos"

Chlorophytum comosum variegatum

STREPTOCALYX POEPPIGI
6-4-3

Description: Broad strap leaves of shiny green; vase-shaped plant.
Size: To 6 feet.
Temperature: 55–75° F.
Humidity: 30–40 per cent.
Watering: Keep evenly moist.
Light: Bright.
Remarks: Good, large bromeliad that lives for years with only reasonable care.

PANDANUS SANDERAE
6-4-3

Description: Swordlike shiny green leaves banded golden yellow.
Size: To 48 inches. (Diameter.)
Temperature: 55–75° F.
Humidity: 20–30 per cent.
Watering: Keep soil somewhat dry.
Light: Bright.
Remarks: Excellent room plant; takes abuse. New plants from offsets at base of mature plants.

PANDANUS VEITCHII
(screw pine) 6-4-3

Description: Variegated recurved leaves.
Size: To 40 inches. (Diameter.)
Temperature: 60–75° F.
Humidity: 30–40 per cent.
Watering: Keep soil somewhat dry.
Light: Bright.
Remarks: Excellent indoors; big but beautiful.

PANDANUS UTILIS
(screw pine) 6-4-3

Description: Long, curving spiny-lance, olive-green leaves.
Size: To 40 inches. (Diameter.)
Temperature: 60–75° F.
Humidity: 30–40 per cent.
Watering: Keep soil somewhat dry.
Light: Bright.
Remarks: A most amenable plant; good table accent.

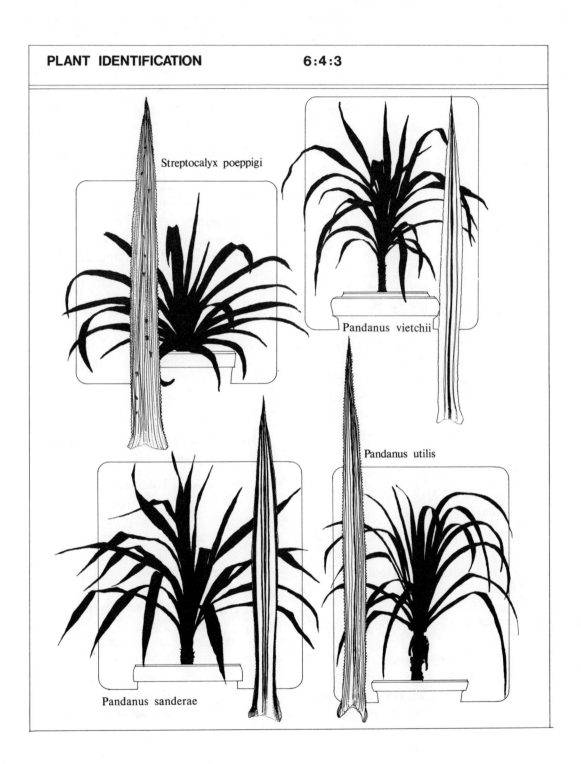

Streptocalyx poeppigi

Pandanus vietchii

Pandanus utilis

Pandanus sanderae

CYPRIPEDIUM HYBRID
(lady-slipper orchid)   7-1-3

Description: Straplike green leaves;
exotic flowers.
Size: To 38 inches.
Temperature: 60–75° F.
Humidity: 40–50 per cent.
Watering: Keep soil evenly moist.
Light: Bright.
Remarks: Terrestrial orchid.
Many varieties, and
most make stunning
houseplants.

BAMBUSA MULTIPLEX NANA
(bamboo)   7-1-3

Description: Grassy foliage; small
leaves, and graceful.
Size: To 48 inches.
Temperature: 55–70° F.
Humidity: 20–40 per cent.
Watering: Keep soil moist at all
times.
Light: Bright.
Remarks: One of the small
bamboos that does well
indoors; pretty and
graceful.

PHALAENOPSIS AMABILIS
(moth orchid)   7-1-3

Description: Long, dark green strap
leaves; exotic white
flowers.
Size: To 24 inches.
Temperature: 60–75° F.
Humidity: 60–70 per cent.
Watering: Keep potting mix
somewhat dry.
Light: Bright.
Remarks: One of the best
houseplant orchids. Pot
in fir bark. Used as
parent for many
varieties.

AGAVE VICTORIAE-REGINAE
(century plant)   7-1-3

Description: Trunkless; a rosette of
narrow olive-green
leaves penciled white.
Size: To 10 inches.
(Diameter.)
Temperature: 55–75° F.
Humidity: 30–40 per cent.
Watering: Grow somewhat dry.
Light: Sun.
Remarks: Do not expect flowers
from plants indoors.
Slow-growing; adjusts
to almost any
condition. Let grow in
the same pot for years.

126

Cypripedium hybrid

Phalaenopsis amabilis

Bambusa multiplex nana

Agave victoria-reginae

CLIVIA MINIATA
(Kafir lily)   7-1-3

Description: Dark-green strap
leaves to 18 inches;
orange-colored
flowers.

Size: To 30 inches.

Temperature: 55–70° F.

Humidity: 20–30 per cent.

Watering: Water heavily during
growth, not so much
the rest of the year.

Light: Tolerates sun, but does
better in shade.

Remarks: Makes a striking picture
in bloom in April and
May. Leaves are
ornamental, and the
vivid tubular flowers
exciting.

CHLOROPHYTUM BICHETII
(spider plant)   7-1-3

Description: Green-and-white-
striped leaves.

Size: To 60 inches.
(Trailing.)

Temperature: 50–75° F.

Humidity: 20–30 per cent.

Watering: Let soil dry out
between waterings.

Light: Bright.

Remarks: Can be neglected and
still survive. Large pot
is best because roots
quickly fill container.

HIPPEASTRUM HYBRID
(amaryllis)   7-1-3

Description: Dark-green tall leaves,
mammoth funnel-
shaped flowers.

Size: To 40 inches.

Temperature: 60–80° F.

Humidity: 30–40 per cent.

Watering: Keep soil evenly moist
in active growth;
barely moist other
times.

Light: Sun.

Remarks: Distinguished plants
with exquisite large
flowers; many
varieties.

GUZMANIA MONOSTACHIA
7-1-3

Description: Strap-leaved rosette.

Size: To 30 inches.
(Diameter.)

Temperature: 55–75° F.

Humidity: 20–30 per cent.

Watering: Keep evenly moist.

Light: Bright.

Remarks: Red, black, and white
poker-shaped flowers;
an oddity.

128

Clivia miniata

Hippeastrum hybrid

Chlorophytum bitchetii

Guzmania monostachia

VRIESEA SPLENDENS
(flaming sword plant) 7-1-3

Description: Green foliage with mahogany stripes, orange "swords" on erect stems. Natural vase shape.
Size: To 20 inches.
Temperature: 55–75° F.
Humidity: 20–30 per cent.
Watering: Keep "vase" filled with water.
Light: Bright.
Remarks: Feathery colorful plumes that last for several months make these ideal north-window plants.

GUZMANIA VITTATA
7-1-3

Description: Stiff and narrow dark green leaves banded with silver. Natural vase shape.
Size: To 24 inches. (Diameter.)
Temperature: 55–75° F.
Humidity: 20–40 per cent.
Watering: Keep "vase" filled with water.
Light: Bright.
Remarks: Robust bromeliad that does well indoors; carefree.

GUZMANIA ZAHNII
7-1-3

Description: 20-inch rosette of green leaves; red-and-white flowers in summer.
Size: To 20 inches.
Temperature: 55–75° F.
Humidity: 50 per cent.
Watering: Keep evenly moist but not soggy.
Light: Bright.
Remarks: Fine table decoration.

130

Vriesea splendens

Guzmania   vittata

Guzmania   zahni

VALLOTA SPECIOSA
(Scarborough lily)   7-1-3

Description: Clusters of startling funnel-formed red flowers in summer and autumn.
Size: To 24 inches.
Temperature: 50–65° F.
Humidity: 30–40 per cent.
Watering: Keep soil moderately moist except after flowering, then grow not quite so wet for about a month, but never dry out completely.
Light: Bright.
Remarks: Large bulbous plant; perfect accent for a cool place.

RHOEO DISCOLOR
(Moses-in-the-cradle)   7-1-3

Description: Rosette of stiff dark green, almost black, leaves, purple underneath.
Size: To 12 inches.
Temperature: 55–75° F.
Humidity: 20–30 per cent.
Watering: Even moisture.
Light: Bright.
Remarks: Easy plant; will grow in jar of water.

GUZMANIA BERTERONIANA
7-1-3

Description: 20-inch rosette of wine-red leaves; yellow flowers in spring.
Size: To 30 inches.
Temperature: 55–75° F.
Humidity: 50 per cent.
Watering: Keep moist but never soggy.
Light: Bright.
Remarks: Flowers stay colorful for four months.

GUZMANIA MAGNIFICA
7-1-3

Description: Dark green strap leaves; orange bract "flowers."
Size: To 30 inches. (Diameter.)
Temperature: 55–75° F.
Humidity: 20–30 per cent.
Watering: Keep evenly moist.
Light: Bright.
Remarks: Excellent table plant; blooms stay in color for months.

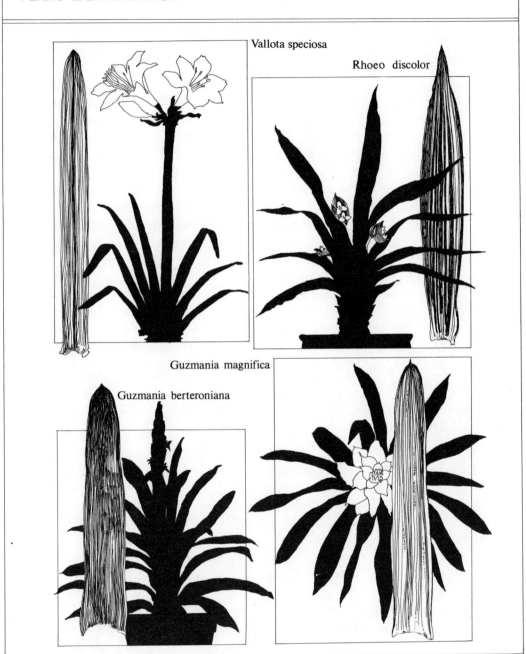

Vallota speciosa

Rhoeo discolor

Guzmania magnifica

Guzmania berteroniana

AECHMEA COELESTIS ALBO-MARGINATA
7-4-3

Description: Leathery gray-green leaves; yellow bracts and blue petals. Natural vase shape.
Size: To 40 inches.
Temperature: 60–75° F.
Humidity: 20–30 per cent.
Watering: Keep "vase" filled with water.
Light: Bright.
Remarks: Pot in fir bark or osmunda; do not feed. New plants from offshoots (stolons) at base.

AECHMEA MARMORATA
(Grecian vase)   7-4-3

Description: Leaves mottled green and maroon; pink bracts and blue flowers. Natural vase shape.
Size: 26–48 inches.
Temperature: 60–75° F.
Humidity: 20–50 per cent.
Watering: Keep "vase" filled with water.
Light: Bright.
Remarks: An excellent bromeliad with dramatic color. Tall and elegant and can take abuse.

CANISTRUM LINDENII VARIEGATUM
7-4-3

Description: Dark green leaves with white stripes.
Size: To 30 inches. Natural vase shape.
Temperature: 60–75° F.
Humidity: 20–40 per cent.
Watering: Keep "vase" filled with water.
Light: Bright.
Remarks: Dramatic plant; excellent for desk or table accent.

AECHMEA FILICAULIS
7-4-3

Description: Grass-green, strap-shaped leaves, and white flowers. Natural vase shape.
Size: 20–30 inches.
Temperature: 60–75° F.
Humidity: 20–30 per cent.
Watering: Keep "vase" filled with water.
Light: Bright.
Remarks: Pot in fir bark or osmunda. A spindly plant but easy to grow.

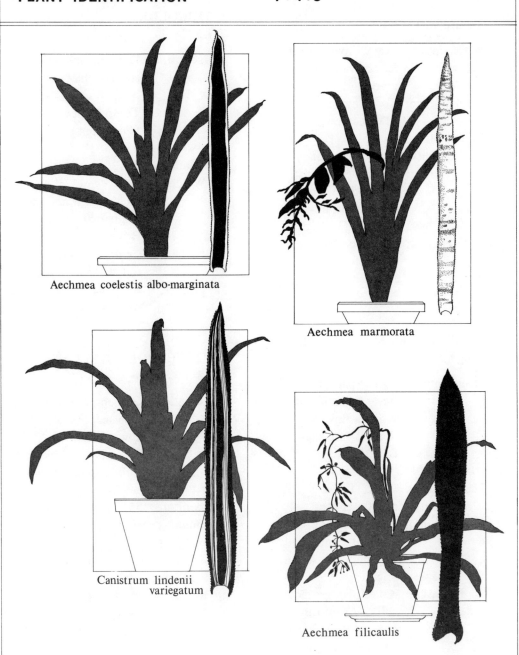

Aechmea coelestis albo-marginata

Aechmea marmorata

Canistrum lindenii
variegatum

Aechmea filicaulis

CRYPTANTHUS ZONATUS
(star plant)   7-4-3

Description: Wavy brown-green
leaves with silver
markings.
Size: To 12 inches.
(Diameter.)
Temperature: 55–75° F.
Humidity: 20–30 per cent.
Watering: Keep evenly moist.
Can endure droughts
for months, however.
Light: Bright.
Remarks: Lovely decorative
accent for terrariums
and dish gardens.

NEOREGELIA SPECTABILIS
(fingernail plant)   7-4-3

Description: Tips of pale green
leaves are brilliant red.
Summer flowering.
Natural vase shape.
Size: To 30 inches.
(Diameter.)
Temperature: 55–75° F.
Humidity: 20–30 per cent.
Watering: Keep "vase" of plant
filled with water and
the compost just damp.
Light: Bright.
Remarks: Makes planters glow
with color for three
months. New plants
from offsets at base of
mature plant.

NEOREGELIA CAROLINAE
TRICOLOR
7-4-3

Description: Dark green leaves
striped white and rose.
Natural vase shape.
Size: To 36 inches.
(Diameter.)
Temperature: 55–75° F.
Humidity: 20–30 per cent.
Watering: Keep "vase" of plant
filled with water and
soil barely damp.
Light: Bright.
Remarks: Center of plant turns
red at bloom time.
Keep leaves clean;
wipe with damp cloth.

HOHENBERGIA STELLATA
7-4-3

Description: Golden-green leaves in
vase shape; violet
flower head.
Size: Rosettes to 48 inches
across, spikes to 40
inches.
Temperature: 55–75° F.
Humidity: 30–50 per cent.
Watering: Keep "vase" of plant
filled with water.
Light: Sun.
Remarks: Plant is spiny, so wear
gloves when handling
it. Good room accent
where there is plenty of
space.

136

Cryptanthus zonatus

Neoregelia carolinae tricolor

Neoregelia spectabilis

Hohenbergia stellata

flecked with silver,
cascading stem of rose
bracts, usually in
summer.

Size: To 40 inches.
Temperature: 55–75° F.
Humidity: 20–30 per cent.
Watering: Keep vase filled with
water.
Light: Bright.
Remarks: Flowers are small, but
the colorful bracts are
striking. Good for
planters in public
places.

AECHMEA FASCIATA
(living-vase plant)   7-4-3

Description: Tufted blue-and-pink
flower heads in spring.
Natural vase shape.
Size: To 24 inches.
Temperature: 60–75° F.
Humidity: 20–30 per cent.
Watering: Keep "vase" filled with
water.
Light: Bright.
Remarks: Pot in fir bark or
osmunda; do not
fertilize. When flowers
fade, offshoots appear
at the base of plants.
Cut them off when they
are two to four inches
high, and pot
separately.

NEOREGELIA CAROLINAE
(fingernail plant)   7-4-3

Description: Dark-green-and-
copper leaves and 30-
to 40-inch leaf rosettes;
winter blooming.
Size: To 36 inches.
(Diameter.)
Temperature: 55–75° F.
Humidity: 20–30 per cent.
Watering: Keep "vase" of plant
filled with water and
the soil just damp.
Light: Bright.
Remarks: Center of plant turns
brilliant red at bloom
time, but flowers are in-
significant. Wipe leaves
with damp cloth about
once a month.

BILLBERGIA ZEBRINA
(living-vase plant)   7-4-3

Description: Gray-green foliage

Billbergia zebrina

Aechmea fasciata

Neoregelia carolinae

CORDYLINE TERMINALIS TRICOLOR
(Ti-plant)   8-1-1

Description: Sword-shaped dark green leaves, lined white and rose.
Size: To 30 inches. (Diameter.)
Temperature: 55–75° F.
Humidity: 20–30 per cent.
Watering: Keep soil evenly moist.
Light: Bright.
Remarks: A cluster plant that grows easily, even in adverse conditions. Colorful foliage makes it fine accent for table or desk.

PHILODENDRON CANNIFOLIUM
8-1-1

Description: Leathery lance-shaped dark green leaves.
Size: To 48 inches. (Vining.)
Temperature: 60–75° F.
Humidity: 30–40 per cent
Watering: Keep soil evenly moist.
Light: Bright.
Remarks: A handsome room plant; needs wood support.

Cordyline terminalis tricolor

Philodendron cannifolium

TRICHOPILIA SUAVIS
8-1-3

Description: Solitary broad leathery green leaves, 5-inch white flowers.
Size: To 20 inches.
Temperature: 55–75° F.
Humidity: 40–50 per cent.
Watering: Allow to be somewhat dry three weeks before and three weeks after blooming.
Light: Bright.
Remarks: An excellent easy-to-grow orchid, with stunning flowers.

CATTLEYA HYBRID
8-1-3

Description: Leathery green spatula leaves.
Size: To 40 inches.
Temperature: 55–75° F.
Humidity: 30–50 per cent.
Watering: Water thoroughly; allow to dry before watering again.
Light: Sun.
Remarks: Some 2,500 varieties. Grow in osmunda or fir bark. Large plants can be divided for new plants.

STANHOPEA OCULATA
(Cow's-horn orchid)   8-1-3

Description: Three to seven 6-inch flowers, usually yellow with orange.
Size: To 36 inches.
Temperature: 60–80° F.
Humidity: 70 per cent.
Watering: Plenty of water all year.
Light: Sun in winter and spring; some shade in summer and fall.
Remarks: Grow this epiphyte in osmunda in slatted redwood basket.

142

Cattleya hybrid

Trichopilia suavis

Stanhopea oculata

ANTHURIUM SCHERZERIANUM
(flamingo flower)　8-2-1

Description: Red flowers.
Size: To 16 inches.
Temperature: 65–80° F.
Humidity: 80 per cent.
Watering: Keep soil evenly moist.
Light: Shaded.
Remarks: Most familiar anthurium. A favorite for arrangements.

BEGONIA ALBO-PICTA
8-2-1

Description: Fibrous, shrubby, branched, and compact. Small glossy green and silvery spotted leaves; small greenish-white flowers.
Size: To 16 inches.
Temperature: 65–75° F.
Humidity: 30–40 per cent.
Watering: Water, allow to dry before watering again.
Light: Bright.
Remarks: Good small angel wing-type begonia for indoors.

CALATHEA BACHEMIANA
8-2-1

Description: Gray-green leaves marked dark green.
Size: To 16 inches.
Temperature: 60–80° F.
Humidity: 80 per cent.
Watering: Plenty of water.
Light: Bright.
Remarks: Fine foliage plant from Brazil. Not easy to grow, but worth extra care for the beautiful foliage.

144

Anthurium scherzerianum

Calathea bachemiana

Begonia albo-picta

ALPINIA SANDERAE
(ginger)   8-2-1

Description: Pale green leaves
edged white.
Size: To 16 inches.
Temperature: 50–70° F.
Humidity: 50 per cent.
Watering: Keep soil evenly moist.
Light: Shade.
Remarks: Good ornamental
plant. From the South
Seas and New Guinea.

HEDYCHIUM GARDNERIANUM
(kahili ginger)   8-2-1

Description: 18-inch dark green
leaves; red-and-yellow
flamboyant blooms.
Size: To 6 feet.
Temperature: 55–75° F.
Humidity: 50 per cent.
Watering: Keep soil very moist.
Light: Sun.
Remarks: Excellent for tubs in a
sunny corner or
outdoors on a terrace.

HEDYCHIUM CORONARIUM
(ginger-lily)   8-2-1

Description: Sweetly scented pure
white flowers; bright
green lance-shaped
leaves.
Size: To 6 feet.
Temperature: 55–75° F.
Humidity: 50 per cent.
Watering: Keep soil very moist;
reduce moisture after
blooming is over.
Light: Sun.
Remarks: Excellent for tubs in a
sunny corner or
outdoors on a terrace.
Divide tubers in spring
for new plants.

BEGONIA LIMMINGHEIANA
8-2-1

Description: Light green leaves with
wavy margins.
Size: To 48 inches.
(Trailing.)
Temperature: 60–75° F.
Humidity: 40–50 per cent.
Watering: Water, allow to dry
before watering again.
Light: Bright.
Remarks: One of the best trailing
plants for baskets.

146

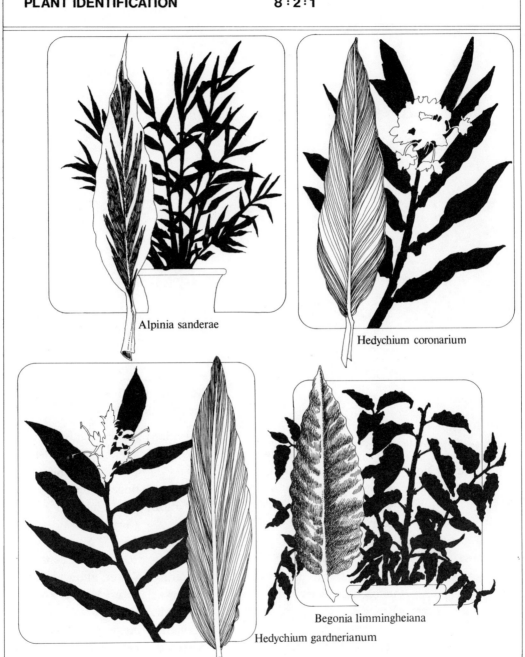

Alpinia sanderae

Hedychium coronarium

Hedychium gardnerianum

Begonia limmingheiana

BEGONIA LUCERNA
(angel-wing begonia)   8-5-2

Description: Large green leaves
spotted silver; giant
flowers.
Size: To 60 inches.
Temperature: 60–75° F.
Humidity: 20–40 per cent.
Watering: Water; allow to dry
before watering again.
Light: Bright.
Remarks: A tall cane-type
begonia; floriferous
and always charming.

BEGONIA ARGENTEO-GUTTATA
(trout begonia)   8-5-2

Description: Strong and branching.
White-speckled leaves;
flowers are white,
tinged pink.
Size: To 16 inches.
(Trailing.)
Temperature: 65–75° F.
Humidity: 30 to 40 per cent.
Watering: Water; allow to dry
before watering again.
Light: Bright.
Remarks: Angel-wing type; nice,
but somewhat difficult
to grow.

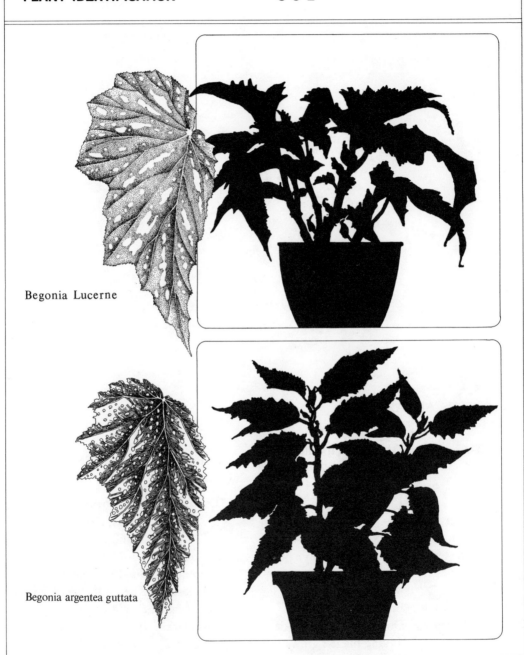

Begonia Lucerne

Begonia argentea guttata

CISSUS ANTARTICA
(kangaroo ivy)   8-5-2

Description:	Dark green toothed leaves.
Size:	To 48 inches. (Trailing.)
Temperature:	55–75° F.
Humidity:	20–30 per cent.
Watering:	Water thoroughly; allow to dry before watering again.
Light:	Bright.
Remarks:	One of the best indoor trailing plants; grows fast.

CLERODENDRUM BUNGEI
(glory bower)   8-5-2

Description:	Large oval felted leaves; red flowers.
Size:	To 60 inches.
Temperature:	50–75° F.
Humidity:	30–40 per cent.
Watering:	Keep soil evenly moist.
Light:	Bright.
Remarks:	A big shrubby plant; makes excellent room plant.

Cissus antartica

Clerodendrum bungei

ALOE VARIEGATA
(partridge-breast aloe)   8-5-3

    Description: Rosette of three-
                cornered, dark rich
                green leaves marbled
                and margined white.
        Size: To 12 inches.
                (Diameter.)
  Temperature: 55–75° F.
     Humidity: 20–30 per cent.
     Watering: Keep soil barely moist.
        Light: Bright.
     Remarks: Very handsome robust
                window plant.

ALOE BREVIFOLIA
8-5-3

    Description: 3- to 4-inch gray-green
                rosette.
        Size: 3–4 inches.
                (Diameter.)
  Temperature: 55–75° F.
     Humidity: 20–30 per cent.
     Watering: Keep soil barely moist.
        Light: Bright.
     Remarks: Occasionally bears a
                tall spike of red flowers
                in late fall.

ALOE CILIARIS
8-5-3

    Description: Soft, green-white,
                toothed leaves with
                sprawling growth and
                pencil stems.
        Size: To 12 inches.
                (Diameter.)
  Temperature: 55–75° F.
     Humidity: 20–30 per cent.
     Watering: Keep soil barely moist.
        Light: Bright.
     Remarks: Ungainly, but easy to
                grow; good window
                plant.

ALOE ARBORESCENS
(candelabra aloe)   8-5-3

    Description: Thick blue-green
                leaves.
        Size: To 10 feet.
                (Diameter.)
  Temperature: 55–75° F.
     Humidity: 20–30 per cent.
     Watering: Keep soil barely moist.
        Light: Bright.
     Remarks: A giant for outdoor
                tubs; baby plants
                appear at base of
                mature plants.

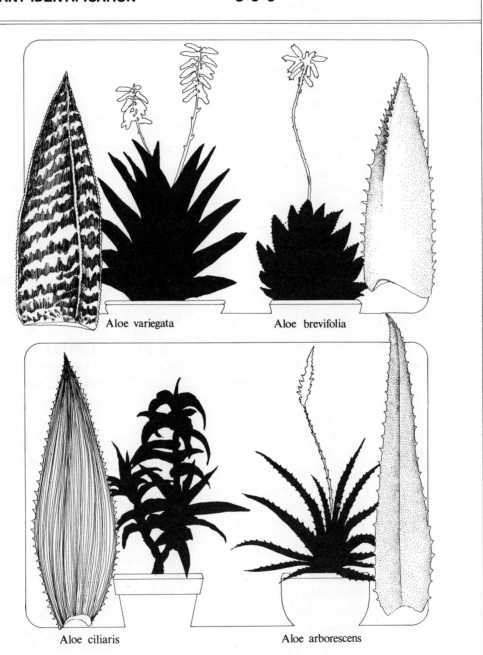

Aloe variegata

Aloe brevifolia

Aloe ciliaris

Aloe arborescens

PASSIFLORA CAERULEA
(passion flower)   9-1-2

Description: Large-lobed green
leaves; dark blue-and-
pink flowers.
Size: To 6 feet. (Vine.)
Temperature: 55–75° F.
Humidity: 40–50 per cent.
Watering: Plenty of water and
fertilizer when actively
growing.
Light: Sun.
Remarks: Too large for windows,
but excellent for plant
room or sun porch.

HEDERA CANARIENSIS
(Algerian ivy)   9-1-2

Description: Large, fresh green,
leathery leaves, slightly
recurved.
Size: 1–5 feet. (Vine.)
Temperature: 50–60° F.
Humidity: 30–50 per cent.
Watering: Soak soil, let dry, then
soak again. Give
overhead spraying in
the sink at least once a
week.
Light: Bright.
Remarks: Bright decoration for
brick walls in a plant
room, in baskets, or
trained in topiary
form. New plants from
cuttings any time.

PASSIFLORA TRIFASCIATA
(passion flower)   9-1-2

Description: Glowing purple-and-
green foliage; blue
flowers.
Size: To 6 feet. (Vine.)
Temperature: 55–75° F.
Humidity: 40–50 per cent.
Watering: Plenty of water during
growing period; not so
much at other times.
Light: Sun.
Remarks: Exquisite large summer
or fall flowers. Take
cuttings in summer for
spring growing.

SYNGONIUM WENDLANDII
(arrowhead)   9-1-2

Description: Dainty creeper, with
dark green white-
veined leaves.
Size: To 30 inches.
Temperature: 55–75° F.
Humidity: 30–40 per cent.
Watering: Keep evenly moist.
Light: Bright or shade.
Remarks: Desirable old-
fashioned pot plant.

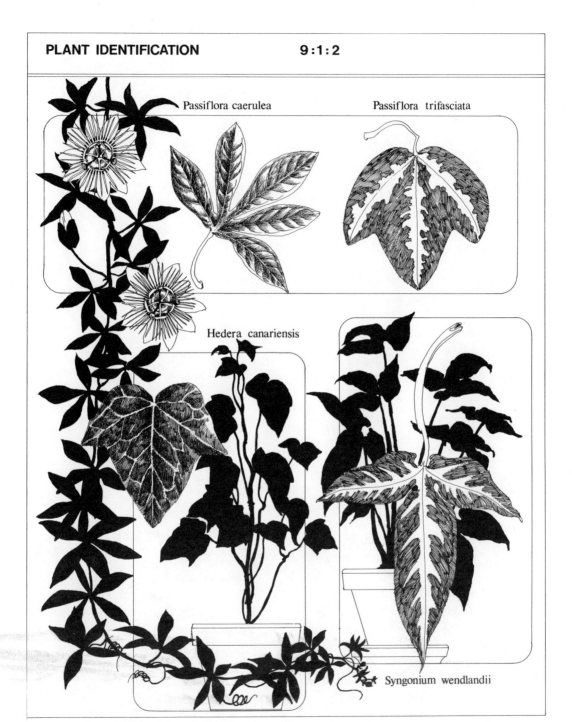

Passiflora caerulea

Passiflora trifasciata

Hedera canariensis

Syngonium wendlandii

BEGONIA CLEOPATRA
(maple-leaf begonia)   9-5-2

Description: Light green leaves with brown areas; pink flowers.
Size: To 30 inches.
Temperature: 58–65° F.
Humidity: 30–40 per cent.
Watering: Keep soil evenly moist.
Light: Bright.
Remarks: Fine window or hanging plant. Can take abuse.

PELARGONIUM GLUTINOSUM
(pheasant's-foot geranium)   9-5-2

Description: Hairy, deeply lobed leaves; pungent.
Size: To 28 inches.
Temperature: 50–70° F.
Humidity: 20–30 per cent.
Watering: Keep soil evenly moist.
Light: Bright.
Remarks: Charming small plant for windowsill.

Begonia Cleopatra

Pelargonium glutinosum

PELARGONIUM
ODORATISSIMUM
(geranium)   9-5-2

Description: Tiny leaves; miniature,
with apple scent.
Size: To 20 inches.
Temperature: 50–70° F.
Humidity: Low.
Watering: Avoid overwatering,
and do not mist the
foliage.
Light: Bright.
Remarks: Good scented type;
nice for kitchen.

SAXIFRAGA SARMENTOSA
(strawberry geranium)   9-5-2

Description: Soft and fleshy,
rounded olive green
leaves with short hairs.
Size: To 20 inches.
(Trailing.)
Temperature: 60–75° F.
Humidity: 20–30 per cent.
Watering: Water; allow to dry
before watering again.
Light: Bright.
Remarks: A fine all-around
houseplant. New plants
from "runners".

Pelargonium odoratissiumum

Saxifraga sarmentosa

CLERODENDRUM SPECIOSUM
(glory bower)   10-1-1

Description: Lush green foliage,
with rose-pink flowers
in summer.
Size: To 6 feet.
Temperature: 50–65° F.
Humidity: 30–40 per cent.
Watering: Keep soil evenly moist,
except in winter.
Light: Sun.
Remarks: Decorative as pot plant
or in baskets. Wealth
of color for little effort.

CTENANTHE LUBBERSIANA
10-1-1

Description: Yellow-mottled green
leaves.
Size: To 24 inches.
Temperature: 55–75° F.
Humidity: 50–60 per cent.
Watering: Keep soil evenly moist.
Light: Bright.
Remarks: Fine foliage plant, with
stiff upright variegated
leaves.

DIPLADENIA AMOENA
(Mexican love vine)   10-1-1

Description: Dark green oblong
leaves; 2-inch pink
flowers.
Size: To 3 feet. (Trailing.)
Temperature: 60–80° F.
Humidity: 50 per cent.
Watering: Keep soil moist, except
immediately after
flowering, then carry
somewhat dry for
about six weeks.
Light: Bright.
Remarks: Great displays of pale
pink flowers in spring
and summer,
sometimes into fall.

SCHEFFLERA ACTINOPHYLLA
(umbrella plant)   10-1-1

Description: Fast growing, with
large palmate leaves;
greenish flowers.
Size: To 60 inches.
Temperature: 55–75° F.
Humidity: 20–30 per cent.
Watering: Water only once or
twice a week.
Light: Bright.
Remarks: Well-grown specimen
becomes handsome
tree.

Dipladenia amoena

Clerodendrum speciosum

Ctenanthe lubbersiana

Schefflera actinophylla

HOFFMANNIA ROEZLII
11-1-1

Description: Copper-brown-and-bronze foliage.
Size: To 30 inches.
Temperature: 50–75° F.
Humidity: 40–50 per cent.
Watering: Keep soil evenly moist.
Light: Shade.
Remarks: Good for planters and color accents.

CRASSULA ARGENTEA
(jade tree)   11-1-1

Description: Branching stems of glossy leaves.
Size: To 5 feet.
Temperature: 55–75° F.
Humidity: 20–30 per cent.
Watering: Let soil dry out between waterings.
Light: Bright or sun.
Remarks: An ideal houseplant. Tolerates lack of moisture in air and soil.

ECHEVERIA PULVINATA
(chenille plant)   11-1-1

Description: Thick ash-green, red-lined leaves with silver hairs.
Size: To 30 inches.
Temperature: 55–75° F.
Humidity: 20–40 per cent.
Watering: Keep soil evenly moist.
Light: Bright.
Remarks: Rosette form; fine table plant. Propagate from offshoots.

ECHEVERIA GLAUCA
11-1-1

Description: Bluish-gray rosettes.
Size: To 30 inches.
Temperature: 55–75° F.
Humidity: 20–30 per cent.
Watering: Keep soil somewhat dry.
Light: Bright.
Remarks: Flowers appear in spring and summer.

162

Echeveria pulvinata

Hoffmannia roezlii

Echeveria glauca

Crassula argentea

HOFFMANNIA REFULGENS
11-1-1

Description: Almost iridescent crinkled leaves, edged with magenta and rose.
Size: To 15 inches.
Temperature: 50–75° F.
Humidity: 40–50 per cent.
Watering: Keep soil evenly moist.
Light: Shade.
Remarks: Good for planters and bright accents. New plants from cuttings.

CRASSULA PORTULACEA
11-1-1

Description: Fleshy, small pointed leaves.
Size: To 48 inches.
Temperature: 55–75° F.
Humidity: 20–30 per cent.
Watering: Water; allow to dry before watering again.
Light: Bright.
Remarks: Somewhat like *C. argentea;* good indoor grower.

PITTISPORUM TOBIRA
11-1-1

Description: Thick and leathery dark green leaves.
Size: To 48 inches.
Temperature: 55–75° F.
Humidity: 20–30 per cent.
Watering: Water; allow to dry before watering again.
Light: Shade.
Remarks: Good tub plant; wash foliage frequently with damp cloth.

Hoffmannia refulgens

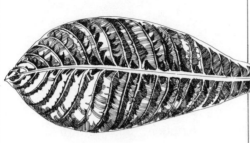

Pittisporum tobira

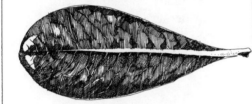

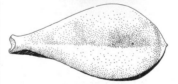

Crassula portulacea

BEGONIA FOLIOSA
(fernleaf begonia)   11-6-2

Description: Pendent branches,
with tiny bronze-green
oval leaves.
Size: To 30 inches.
(Trailing.)
Temperature: 55–75° F.
Humidity: 20–40 per cent.
Watering: Plenty of water.
Light: Bright.
Remarks: A charming begonia,
best grown in basket.

PILEA INVOLUCRATA
(aluminum plant)   11-6-2

Description: Bushy brown leaves;
rose-red blooms.
Size: To 12 inches or more.
Temperature: 50–75° F.
Humidity: 30–40 per cent.
Watering: Keep soil moist.
Light: Bright.
Remarks: Popular terrarium or
dish-garden plant.
New plants from
cuttings.

PILEA CADIEREI
(aluminum plant)   11-6-2

Description: Silver and green
foliage; rose-red
flowers.
Size: To 12 inches or more.
Temperature: 50–75° F.
Humidity: 30–40 per cent.
Watering: Keep soil moist.
Light: Bright.
Remarks: Fine terrarium subject;
grows readily.

KALANCHOE FEDTSCHENKOI
11-6-2

Description: Small, fleshy, metallic-
green leaves.
Size: To 28 inches.
Temperature: 55–75° F.
Humidity: 20–30 per cent.
Watering: Water; allow to dry
before watering again.
Light: Bright.
Remarks: Good bushy succulent
for windows. New
plants from offsets.

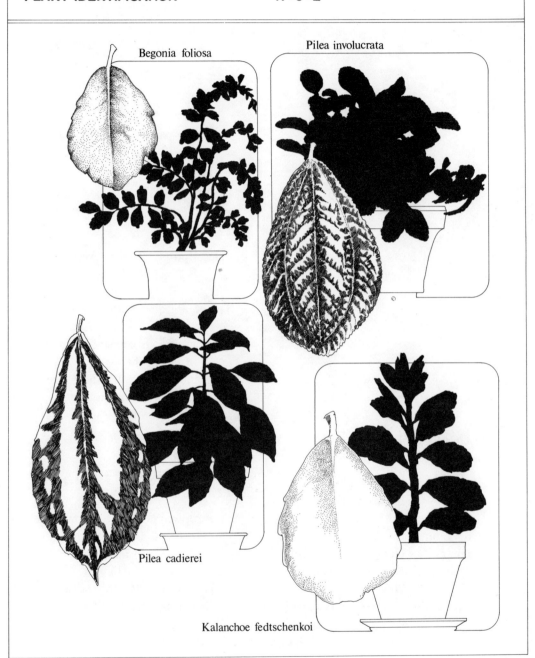

Begonia foliosa

Pilea involucrata

Pilea cadierei

Kalanchoe fedtschenkoi

PHILODENDRON CRUENTUM
12-1-1

Description: 8-inch leaves.
Size: To 20 inches.
(Vining.)
Temperature: 55–75° F.
Humidity: 20–30 per cent.
Watering: Keep soil evenly moist.
Light: Shade.
Remarks: Small vining-type philodendron for windows.

ALOCASIA ZEBRINA
12-1-1

Description: Green leaves with brown zebra bands.
Size: To 18 inches.
Temperature: 65–75° F.
Humidity: High, to 80 per cent.
Watering: Keep soil moist.
Light: Shade.
Remarks: Dramatic exotic, with showy velvety green foliage. Needs perfect drainage.

PHILODENDRON HASTATUM
12-1-1

Description: 10-inch arrow leaves.
Size: To 36 inches.
(Vining.)
Temperature: 55–75° F.
Humidity: 20–30 per cent.
Watering: Keep soil evenly moist.
Light: Shade.
Remarks: Handsome accent plant that grows easily.

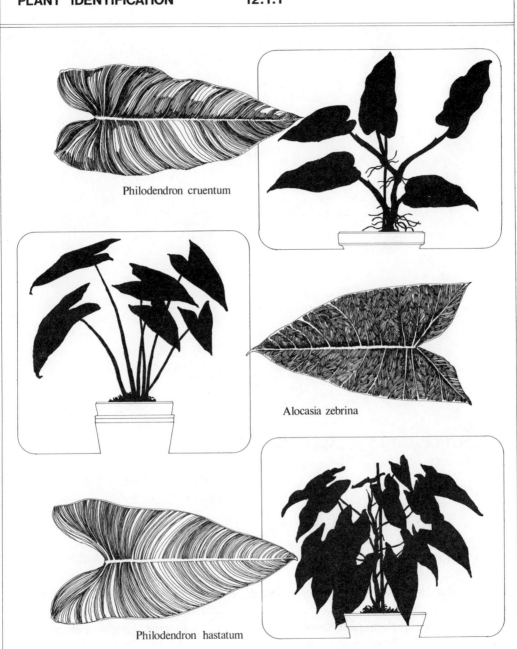

Philodendron cruentum

Alocasia zebrina

Philodendron hastatum

ANTHURIUM CRYSTALLINUM
(flamingo flower)   12-1-1

Description:	Velvety green leaves, silver veined; insignificant flowers.
Size:	To 14 inches.
Temperature:	65–80° F.
Humidity:	To 80 per cent.
Watering:	Keep soil evenly moist.
Light:	Shade.
Remarks:	Perhaps the most handsome of the anthuriums.

PHILODENDRON ERUBESCENS
12-1-1

Description:	10-inch dark-green leaves.
Size:	To 24 inches. (Vining.)
Temperature:	55–75° F.
Humidity:	20–30 per cent.
Watering:	Keep soil evenly moist.
Light:	Shade.
Remarks:	Good table plant.

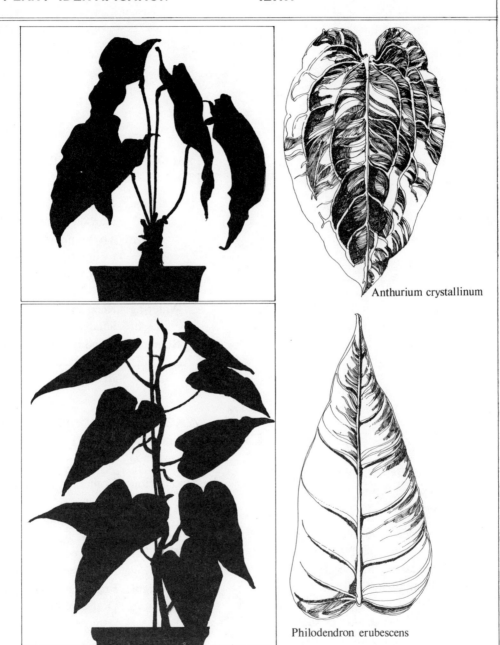

Anthurium crystallinum

Philodendron erubescens

PHILODENDRON IMBE
12-1-1

Description: 10-inch leathery
maroon leaves.
Size: To 24 inches.
(Vining.)
Temperature: 55–75° F.
Humidity: 20–30 per cent.
Watering: Keep soil evenly moist.
Light: Shade.
Remarks: Good room plant that
grows easily.

SYNGONIUM PODOPHYLLUM
'Emerald Green'
(arrowhead)   12-1-1

Description: Trailer, with rich green
leaves.
Size: To 30 inches.
Temperature: 55–75° F.
Humidity: 30–40 per cent.
Watering: Keep evenly moist.
Light: Bright or shade.
Remarks: Desirable old-
fashioned pot plant.
Propagate from
cuttings.

SYNGONIUM PODOPHYLLUM
'Imperial White'
(arrowhead)   12-1-1

Description: Greenish-white foliage.
Size: To 30 inches.
Temperature: 55–75° F.
Humidity: 30–40 per cent.
Watering: Keep evenly moist.
Light: Bright or shade.
Remarks: Desirable old-
fashioned pot plant.

172

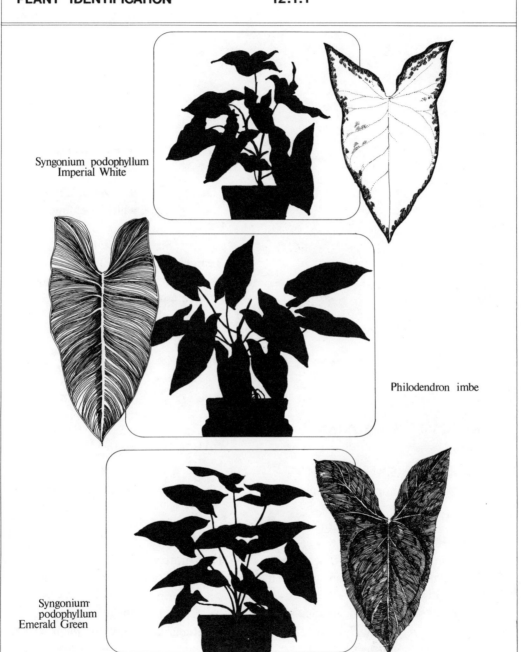

Syngonium podophyllum
Imperial White

Philodendron imbe

Syngonium
podophyllum
Emerald Green

CALADIUM 'Ace of Spades'
12-2-1

Description: Red veins, red-and-
white marbling, green
edges.
Size: 20–30 inches.
Temperature: 60–70° F.
Humidity: 60 per cent or higher.
Watering: Plenty of water.
Light: Shade.
Remarks: Stunning foliage.
Grand summer
decoration for shaded
windows.

ALOCASIA WATSONIANA
12-2-1

Description: Silver veins on
corrugated blue-green
leaves.
Size: To 28 inches.
Temperature: 65–75° F.
Humidity: High, to 80 per cent.
Watering: Keep soil evenly moist.
Light: Shade.
Remarks: Dramatic exotic. The
"queen" of the
alocasias. Needs
perfect drainage.

CALADIUM 'Edith Meade'
12-2-1

Description: Dark-green-and-white
paper-thin leaves, red
veins.
Size: 20–30 inches.
Temperature: 60–70° F.
Humidity: 60 per cent or higher.
Watering: Plenty of water.
Light: Shade.
Remarks: Dramatic plant; group
several together for
fine display.

174

CALADIUM 'Ace of Spades'
12-2-1

Description: Red veins, red-and-white marbling, green edges.
Size: 20–30 inches.
Temperature: 60–70° F.
Humidity: 60 per cent or higher.
Watering: Plenty of water.
Light: Shade.
Remarks: Stunning foliage. Grand summer decoration for shaded windows.

ALOCASIA WATSONIANA
12-2-1

Description: Silver veins on corrugated blue-green leaves.
Size: To 28 inches.
Temperature: 65–75° F.
Humidity: High, to 80 per cent.
Watering: Keep soil evenly moist.
Light: Shade.
Remarks: Dramatic exotic. The "queen" of the alocasias. Needs perfect drainage.

CALADIUM 'Edith Meade'
12-2-1

Description: Dark-green-and-white paper-thin leaves, red veins.
Size: 20–30 inches.
Temperature: 60–70° F.
Humidity: 60 per cent or higher.
Watering: Plenty of water.
Light: Shade.
Remarks: Dramatic plant; group several together for fine display.

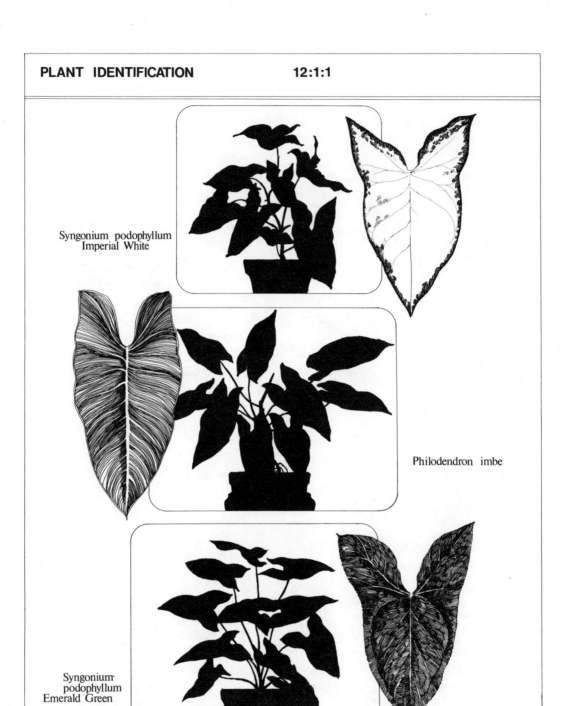

Syngonium podophyllum
Imperial White

Philodendron imbe

Syngonium
podophyllum
Emerald Green

Caladium Ace of Spades

Alocasia watsoniana

Caladium Edith Meade

ALOCASIA AMAZONICA
12-2-1

Description: Bushy, with white-
veined scalloped
leaves.
Size: To 20 inches.
Temperature: 65–75° F.
Humidity: High humidity, to 80
per cent.
Watering: Keep moist.
Light: Shade.
Remarks: Dramatic exotic, with
showy velvety green
foliage. Needs good
drainage.

PHILODENDRON CORDATUM
12-2-1

Description: Heart-shaped leaves;
more leathery than
P. oxycardium.
Size: To 36 inches.
(Vining.)
Temperature: 55–75° F.
Humidity: 20–30 per cent.
Watering: Keep soil evenly moist.
Light: Bright.
Remarks: Generally sold as
P. oxycardium.
Cuttings root easily in
water.

COLOCASIA ANTIQUORUM
ILLUSTRIS
(elephant-ear)   12-2-1

Description: Green foliage with
purple spots.
Size: To 48 inches.
Temperature: 60–80° F.
Humidity: 30–40 per cent.
Watering: Needs plenty of water.
Light: Bright.
Remarks: An elegant plant with
dramatic leaves.
Tropical in
appearance. Divide
tubers in spring for new
plants.

XANTHOSOMA LINDENII
12-2-1

Description: Green-and-white 12-
inch leaves.
Size: To 36 inches.
Temperature: 65–85° F.
Humidity: 70 per cent.
Watering: Evenly moist soil.
Light: Bright.
Remarks: Jungle plants from
South America for that
tropical look. New
plants by dividing
tubers in spring.

Alocasia amazonica

Colocasia antiquorum illustris

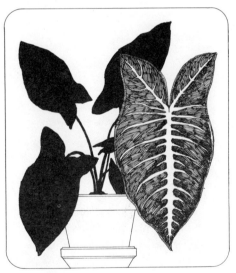

Philodendron cordatum

Xanthosoma lindenii

FITTONIA VERSCHAFFELTII
13-1-1

Description: Low, dense creeper with soft bright green, 4-inch leaves with red veins.
Size: To 26 inches.
Temperature: 60–75° F.
Humidity: 50 per cent.
Watering: Let soil dry out between waterings.
Light: Shade.
Remarks: Keep out of drafts. Grow several kinds of fittonia in one container for a colorful display. New plants from tip cuttings.

MARANTA BICOLOR
13-1-1

Description: Oval dark gray-green foliage.
Size: To 12 inches.
Temperature: 60–80° F.
Humidity: 50 per cent.
Watering: Keep soil evenly moist.
Light: Shade.
Remarks: In fall, cut away old foliage but leave the most recent foliage. Divide mature plants for new ones.

MARANTA LEUCONEURA KERCHOVEANA
(prayer plant)   13-1-1

Description: 6-inch oval glaucous leaves, pale grayish green, with rows of brown and dark green spots.
Size: To 15 inches.
Temperature: 60–80° F.
Humidity: 50 per cent.
Watering: Keep soil evenly moist.
Light: Shade.
Remarks: Folds leaves at night to funnel dew down to the roots.

MARANTA LEUCONEURA MASSANGEANA
(prayer plant)   13-1-1

Description: Small gray-green leaves with silver markings.
Size: To 15 inches.
Temperature: 60–80° F.
Humidity: 50 per cent.
Watering: Keep soil evenly moist.
Light: Shade.
Remarks: Ornamental foliage and excellent grower.

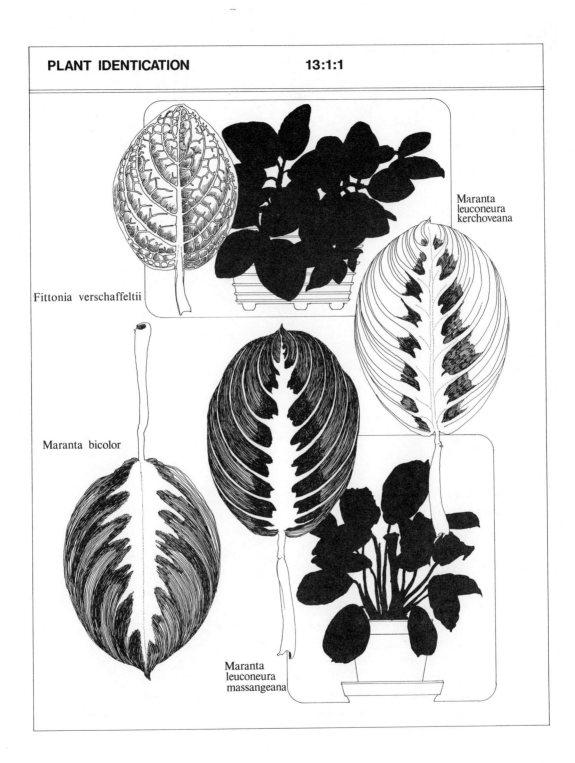

Fittonia verschaffeltii

Maranta
leuconeura
kerchoveana

Maranta bicolor

Maranta
leuconeura
massangeana

FICUS ELASTICA DECORA
(rubber tree)   13-1-1

Description: Thick, glossy green
leaves.
Size: To 5 feet.
Temperature: 60–75° F.
Humidity: 20–30 per cent.
Watering: Keep soil evenly moist;
dry out somewhat in
winter.
Light: Bright.
Remarks: Occasionally wipe
foliage with a damp
cloth and plain water.

PEPEROMIA OBTUSIFOLIA
13-1-1

Description: Fleshy, large oval
leaves.
Size: To 12 inches.
(Vining.)
Temperature: 55–75° F.
Humidity: 20–30 per cent.
Watering: Keep soil evenly moist.
Light: Bright.
Remarks: Outstanding plant for
window, table planter,
or terrarium.

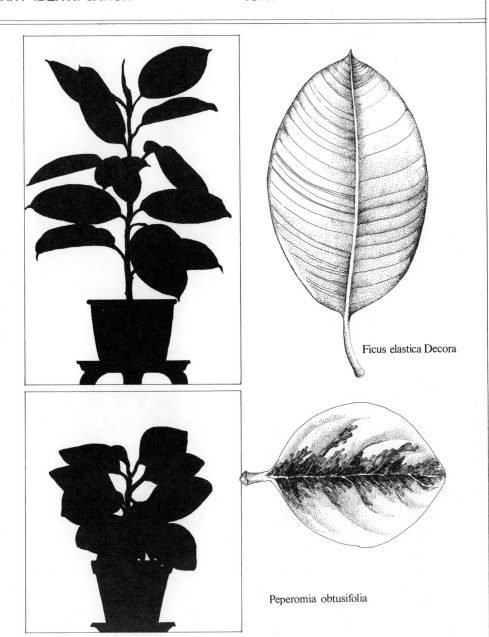

Ficus elastica Decora

Peperomia obtusifolia

SINNINGIA HYBRID
(gloxinia)   13-6-1

Description: Long bluish-green
leaves with sunken
veins and toothed
edges.
Size: To 28 inches.
Temperature: 55–75° F.
Humidity: 40–50 per cent.
Watering: Water; allow to dry
before watering again.
Light: Shade.
Remarks: Many, many varieties
with funnel-shaped
flowers in an array of
colors.

HYPOCYRTA NUMMULARIA
(goldfish plant)   13-6-1

Description: A creeper, with
vermilion-yellow-violet
flowers.
Size: To 24 inches.
(Trailing.)
Temperature: 60–80° F.
Humidity: 60 per cent.
Watering: Keep soil evenly moist.
Light: Sun in winter; shade in
summer.
Remarks: May go dormant in
summer, but leafs out
again in fall.

182

Sinningia hybrid

Hypocyrta nummularia

SAINTPAULIA CONFUSA
14-5-1

Description: Light green thin
leaves.
Size: To 14 inches.
Temperature: 55–75° F.
Humidity: 20–30 per cent.
Watering: Keep moist.
Light: Bright.
Remarks: Often used as parent
for African violet
varieties.

SAINTPAULIA GROTEI
14-5-1

Description: Fresh green ovoid
leaves; violet-blue
flowers.
Size: To 18 inches.
Temperature: 55–75° F.
Humidity: 20–30 per cent.
Watering: Keep moist.
Light: Bright.
Remarks: A trailing African
violet.

SAINTPAULIA INTERMEDIA
14-5-1

Description: Purplish-green leaves;
purple flowers.
Size: To 18 inches.
Temperature: 55–75° F.
Humidity: 20–30 per cent.
Watering: Keep moist.
Light: Bright.
Remarks: Used as parent for
African violet varieties.

Saintpaulia confusa

Saintpaulia intermedia

Saintpaulia grotei

Appendix

Always a welcome sight is the Christmas begonia, a mass of colorful blooms at seasonal time. (*Photo by Roche*)

Hypocyrta, *the goldfish plant, sports orange flowers and is becoming a popular indoor plant.* (*Photo by Merry Gardens*)

188

Where to Buy Plants and Supplies (mail order)

Plants can be purchased from local nurseries or plant shops or, if looking for special species, can be ordered from mail-order suppliers below. There is generally a catalogue charge which may range from $ .25 to $2.00.

Alberts & Merkel Bros., Inc.
P. O. Box 537
Boynton Beach, Florida   33435

Catalogue. Wide selection of flowering plants.

Arthur Eames Allgrove
Box 459
Wilmington, Massachusetts   01887

Unusual selection of many tropical plants. Catalogue free.

Buell's Greenhouses
Eastford, Connecticut   06242

Gesneriads and other flowering plants. Catalogue.

W. Atlee Burpee Company Box 6929 Philadelphia, Pennsylvania 19132	Houseplants of all kinds. Free catalogue.
Cactus Gem Nursery P. O. Box 327 Aromas, California 95004	Good selection of cacti and succulents.
Cactus by Mueller 10411 Rosedale Highway Bakersfield, California 93308	Good selection.
P. DeJaeger & Sons, Inc. 188 Asbury Street South Hamilton, Massachusetts 01982	Outstanding selection of bulbous plants.
Fischer Greenhouses Linwood, New Jersey 08221	African violets and other gesneriads.
Hausermann's Orchids Box 363 Elmhurst, Illinois 60126	Large selection of orchids. Catalogue.
Henrietta's Nursery 1345 North Brawley Fresno, California 93705	Very extensive selection of all kinds of cacti. Twenty cents for catalogue.
Margaret Ilgenfritz Orchids Box 665 Monroe, Michigan 48161	Excellent selection of orchids. Catalogue.
Kartuz Greenhouses 92 Chestnut Street Wilmington, Massachusetts 01887	Fine selection of flowering plants. Catalogue.
Logees Greenhouses 55 North Street Danielson, Connecticut 06239	Wide choice of hard to find houseplants. Catalogue.

Merry Gardens   Hard to find plants; fine selection.
Camden, Maine   04843   Catalogue.

Oak Hill Gardens   Orchids, tropical plants.
P. O. Box 25—Binnie Road
West Dundee, Illinois   60118

George W. Park Seed Co.   Houseplants. Free catalogue.
Greenwood, South Carolina   29646

Tinari Greenhouses   Episcias and other gesneriads.
2325 Valley Road.
Huntington Valley,
Pennsylvania   19006

Index

Echeverias look as if they are carved from jade and they are easy-to-grow indoor plants that soon fill their containers. (Photo by M. Barr)

List of Houseplants by Common Name

Common Name	*Botanical Name*
African violet	*Saintpaulia*
Algerian ivy	*Hedera canariensis*
Aluminum plant	*Pilea involucrata*
Amaryllis	*Hippeastrum hybrid*
Angel's-trumpet	*Datura mollis*
Angel-wing begonia	*Begonia lucerna*
Arrowhead	*Syngonium podophyllum* 'Emerald Green'
Arrowhead	*S. podophyllum* 'Imperial White'
Bamboo	*Bambusa multiplex nana*
Beefsteak begonia	*Begonia erythrophylla*
Cabbage philodendron	*Philodendron wendlandii*
Candelabra aloe	*Aloe arborescens*

Common Name	Botanical Name
Cape jasmine	*Gardenia jasminoides*
Cast-iron plant	*Aspidistra elatior*
Cast-iron plant	*A. e. variegata*
Century plant	*Agave victoriae-reginae*
Chenille plant	*Acalypha godseffiana*
Chenille plant	*A. wilkesiana macrophylla*
Chenille plant	*Echeveria pulvinata*
Chinese evergreen	*Aglaonema commutatum*
Chinese evergreen	*A. pictum*
Chinese evergreen	*A. robelinii*
Christmas begonia	*Begonia cheimantha*
Corn plant	*Dracaena fragrans massangeana*
Corn plant	*D. sanderiana*
Cow's-horn orchid	*Stanhopea oculata*
Creeping fig	*Ficus pumila*
Croton	*Codiaeum gloriosum*
Crown-of-thorns	*Euphorbia splendens*
Decorator plant	*Dracaena marginata*
Dumbcane	*Dieffenbachia amoena*
Dumbcane	*D. hoffmannii*
Dumbcane	*D. splendens*
Dwarf orange tree	*Citrus taitensis*
Elephant-ear	*Colocasia antiquorum illustris*
Eyelash begonia	*Begonia boweri*
Fernleaf begonia	*Begonia foliosa*
Fingernail plant	*Neoregelia spectabilis*
Flame-of-the woods	*Ixora chinensis*
Flamingo flower	*Anthurium andraeanum*
Flamingo flower	*A. crystallinum*
Flamingo flower	*A. scherzerianum*
Flaming sword plant	*Vriesea splendens*
Ginger	*Alpinia sanderae*
Ginger-lily	*Hedychium coronarium*
Glory bower	*Clerodendrum bungei*
Glory bower	*Medinilla magnifica*
Gloxinia	*Sinningia*
Gold-dust plant	*Dracaena godseffiana*
Gold-dust plant	*D. goldieana*

Common Name	Botanical Name
Gold-dust tree	*Aucuba grandifolia*
Goldfish plant	*Hypocyrta nummularia*
Goldfish plant	*H. strigillosa*
Grecian vase	*Aechmea marmorata*
Hardy begonia	*Begonia evansiana*
Hibiscus	*Hibiscus rosa-sinensis*
Ivy arum	*Scindapsus aureus*
Ivy arum	*S. pictus argyraeus*
Jade tree	*Crassula argentea*
Kafir lily	*Clivia miniata*
Kahili ginger	*Hedychium gardnerianum*
Kangaroo ivy	*Cissus antartica*
Lady's-eardrops	Fuchsia hybrid
Lady-slipper orchid	*Cypripedium hybrid*
Lantana	*Lantana camara*
Lipstick vine	*Aeschynanthus lobbianus*
Lipstick vine	*A. pulchrum*
Lipstick vine	*A. speciosus*
Living-vase plant	*Aechmea fasciata*
Living-vase plant	*Billbergia zebrina*
Madagascar jasmine	*Stephanotis floribunda*
Maple-leaf begonia	*Begonia cleopatra*
Mexican love vine	*Dipladenia amoena*
Miniature holly	*Malpighia coccigera*
Moses-in-a-cradle	*Rhoeo discolor*
Moth orchid	*Phalaenopsis amabilis*
Orange jessamine	*Murraea exotica*
Painted-leaf plant	*Coleus blumei*
Partridge-breast aloe	*Aloe variegata*
Passion flower	*Passiflora caerulea*
Passion flower	*P. trifasciata*
Patience plant	*Impatiens holstii*
Peacock plant	*Episicia cupreata*
Penny begonia	*Begonia kellermannii*
Pheasant's-foot geranium	*Pelargonium glutinosum*
Prayer plant	*Maranta leuconeura kerchoveana*
Prayer plant	*M. l. massangeana*
Pussy ears	*Cyanotis kewensis*

Common Name	Botanical Name
Rainbow plant	*Achimenes grandiflora*
Rainbow plant	*A. patens*
Red-hot poker plant	*Guzmania monostachia*
Rosary vine	*Ceropegia woodii*
Rouge plant	*Rivina humilis*
Rubber tree	*Ficus elastica decora*
Scarborough lily	*Vallota speciosa*
Screw pine	*Pandanus utilis*
Screw pine	*P. sanderae*
Screw pine	*P. veitchii*
Snake plant	*Sansevieria hahni*
Spider plant	*Chlorophytum bichetii*
Spider plant	*C. elatum*
Spider plant	*C. comosum variegatum*
Star plant	*Cryptanthus zonatus*
Stonecrop	*Sedum adolphii*
Strawberry begonia	*Saxifraga sarmentosa*
Swedish ivy	*Plectranthus oertendahii*
Sweet olive	*Osmanthus fragrans*
Swiss-cheese plant	*Philodendron pertusum*
Ti-plant	*Cordyline terminalis tricolor*
Trout begonia	*Begonia argenteo-guttata*
Umbrella tree	*Schefflera actinophylla*
Umbrella tree	*S. digitata*
Velvet plant	*Gynura aurantiaca*
Wandering Jew	*Tradescantia albiflora*
Wandering Jew	*Zebrina pendula*
Wax plant	*Hoya bella*
Wax plant	*H. moteskoi*
Weeping fig	*Ficus benjamina*
White crystal orchid	*Coelogyne cristata*
White flag plant	*Spathiphyllum clevelandii*
Zebra plant	*Calathea zebrina*

List of Houseplants by Botanical Name

Botanical Name	Code	Common Name	Page
Agave striata	6-1-1		120
Agave victoriae-reginae	7-1-3	century plant	126
Aglaonema commutatum	3-2-1	Chinese evergreen	94
Aglaonema pictum	3-2-1	Chinese evergreen	94
Aglaonema robelinii	3-1-1	Chinese evergreen	88
Aglaonema simplex	3-2-1	Chinese evergreen	96
Alocasia amazonica	12-2-1		176
Alocasia lowii grandis	1-2-1		60
Alocasia sedeni	1-2-1		60
Alocasia watsoniana	12-2-1		174
Alocasia zebrina	12-1-1		168
Aloe arborescens	8-5-3	candelabra aloe	152
Aloe brevifolia	8-5-3		152
Aloe ciliaris	8-5-3		152
Aloe variegata	8-5-3	partridge-breast aloe	152
Alpinia sanderae	8-2-1	ginger	146
Anthurium andraeanum	1-1-1	flamingo flower	52
Anthurium crystallinum	12-1-1	flamingo flower	170
Anthurium scherzerianum	8-2-1	flamingo flower	144
Aphelandra aurantiaca roezlii	3-1-1		86
Aphelandra chamissoniana	2-2-1	zebra plant	80
Aphelandra squarrosa louisae	2-2-1		78
Aspidistra elatior	2-1-3	cast-iron plant	76
Aspidistra elatior variegata	2-1-3	cast-iron plant	76
Aucuba grandifolia	2-5-1	gold-dust tree	82
Aucuba longifolia	2-5-1		82
Bambusa multiplex nana	7-1-3	bamboo	126
Begonia albo-picta	8-2-1		144
Begonia argenteo-guttata	8-5-2	trout begonia	148
Begonia boweri	3-4-2	eyelash begonia	102
Begonia cheimantha	4-4-2	Christmas begonia	114
Begonia cleopatra	9-5-2	maple-leaf begonia	156
Begonia erythrophylla	4-4-2	beefsteak begonia	116
Begonia evansiana	3-4-2	hardy begonia	102
Begonia foliosa	11-6-2	fernleaf begonia	166
Begonia imperialis	3-4-2		102
Begonia kellermannii	4-4-2	penny begonia	116
Begonia limmingheiana	8-2-1		146

Botanical Name	Code	Common Name	Page
Begonia lucerna	8-5-2	angel-wing begonia	148
Begonia mazae	4-4-2		116
Begonia metallica	3-4-2		102
Begonia paulensis	4-4-2		116
Billbergia zebrina	7-4-3	living-vase plant	138
Caladium 'Ace of Spades'	12-2-1		174
Caladium 'Ann Greer'	1-2-1		60
Caladium 'Edith Meade'	12-2-1		174
Calathea bachemiana	8-2-1		144
Calathea concinna	3-1-1		84
Calathea leopardina	3-2-1		94
Calathea picturata argentea	2-2-1		78
Calathea roseo-picta	2-2-1		78
Calathea veitchiana	3-1-1		86
Calathea zebrina	2-2-1	zebra plant	78
Camellia japonica	3-4-1		100
Canistrum lindenii variegatum	7-4-3		134
Cattleya hybrid	8-1-3		142
Ceropegia woodii	1-1-1	rosary vine	54
Chlorophytum bichetii	7-1-3	spider plant	128
Chlorophytum comosum variegatum	6-1-3	spider plant	122
Cissus antartica	8-5-2	kangaroo ivy	150
Citrus taitensis	2-1-1	dwarf orange tree	66
Clerodendrum bungei	8-5-2	glory bower	150
Clerodendrum speciosum	10-1-1	glory bower	160
Clerodendrum thomsonae	3-1-1	glory bower	84
Clivia miniata	7-1-3	Kafir lily	128
Codiaeum gloriosum	2-1-1	croton	66
Coelogyne cristata	6-1-3	white crystal orchid	122
Coleus blumei	3-6-1	painted-leaf plant	108
Colocasia antiquorum illustris	12-2-1	elephant ear	176
Cordyline terminalis tricolor	8-1-1	ti-plant	140
Crassula argentea	11-1-1	jade plant	162
Crassula orbicularis	2-1-1		66
Crassula portulacea	11-1-1		164
Crossandra infundibuliformis	2-1-1		70
Cryptanthus zonatus	7-4-3	star plant	136
Ctenanthe lubbersiana	10-1-1		160

Botanical Name	Code	Common Name	Page
Ctenanthe oppenheimiana	2-1-1		68
Cyanotis kewensis	2-1-3	pussy ears	74
Cymbidium 'Dos Pueblos'	6-1-3		122
Cypripedium hybrid	7-1-3		126
Datura mollis	3-2-1	angel's-trumpet	96
Dieffenbachia amoena	2-1-1	dumbcane	68
Dieffenbachia hoffmannii	3-2-1	dumbcane	94
Dieffenbachia splendens	2-2-1	dumbcane	80
Dipladenia amoena	10-1-1	Mexican love vine	160
Dracaena fragrans massangeana	2-1-3	corn plant	76
Dracaena godseffiana	3-1-1	gold-dust plant	86
Dracaena goldieana	3-1-3		90
Dracaena marginata	6-1-1	decorator plant	120
Dracaena sanderiana	2-1-3	corn plant	74
Echeveria glauca	11-1-1		162
Echeveria pulvinata	11-1-1	chenille plant	162
Episcia cupreata	3-6-1	peacock plant	106
Euphorbia splendens	5-1-1	crown-of-thorns	118
Ficus benjamina	2-1-1	weeping fig	64
Ficus elastica decora	13-1-1	rubber tree	180
Ficus pumila	1-1-1	creeping fig	56
Fittonia verschaffeltii	13-1-1		178
Fuchsia hybrid	3-4-1	lady's-eardrops	100
Gardenia jasminoides	2-1-1	cape jasmine	68
Guzmania berteroniana	7-1-3		132
Guzmania magnifica	7-1-3		132
Guzmania monostachia	7-1-3	red-hot poker plant	128
Guzmania vittata	7-1-3		130
Guzmania zahnii	7-1-3		130
Gynura aurantiaca	3-5-1	velvet plant	104
Hedera canariensis	9-1-2	Algerian ivy	154
Hedychium coronarium	8-2-1	ginger-lily	146
Hedychium gardnerianum	8-2-1	kahili ginger	146
Hibiscus rosa-sinensis	3-5-1	hibiscus	104
Hippeastrum hybrid	7-1-3	amaryllis	128
Hoffmannia ghiesbreghtii	2-1-1		70
Hoffmannia refulgens	11-1-1		164
Hoffmannia roezlii	11-1-1		162